Spanish Voices 1

Authentic Listening and Reading Practice in Spanish from Around Latin America and Spain

lingualism

Table of Contents

Accompanying audio and online resources are available at:

www.lingualism.com/sv1

All segments from *Spanish Voices 1* and *Spanish Voices 2*

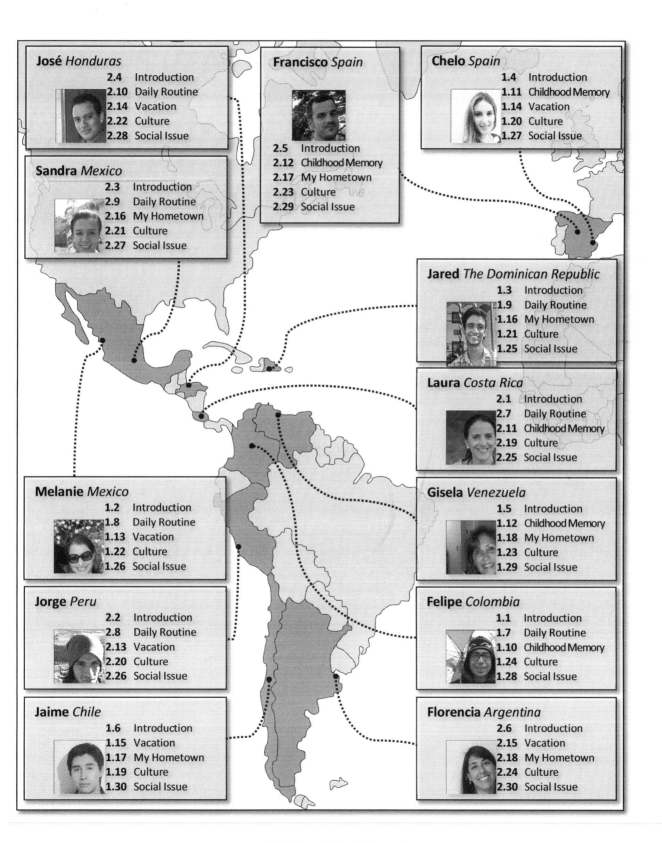

José *Honduras*
2.4 Introduction
2.10 Daily Routine
2.14 Vacation
2.22 Culture
2.28 Social Issue

Sandra *Mexico*
2.3 Introduction
2.9 Daily Routine
2.16 My Hometown
2.21 Culture
2.27 Social Issue

Francisco *Spain*
2.5 Introduction
2.12 Childhood Memory
2.17 My Hometown
2.23 Culture
2.29 Social Issue

Chelo *Spain*
1.4 Introduction
1.11 Childhood Memory
1.14 Vacation
1.20 Culture
1.27 Social Issue

Jared *The Dominican Republic*
1.3 Introduction
1.9 Daily Routine
1.16 My Hometown
1.21 Culture
1.25 Social Issue

Laura *Costa Rica*
2.1 Introduction
2.7 Daily Routine
2.11 Childhood Memory
2.19 Culture
2.25 Social Issue

Melanie *Mexico*
1.2 Introduction
1.8 Daily Routine
1.13 Vacation
1.22 Culture
1.26 Social Issue

Gisela *Venezuela*
1.5 Introduction
1.12 Childhood Memory
1.18 My Hometown
1.23 Culture
1.29 Social Issue

Jorge *Peru*
2.2 Introduction
2.8 Daily Routine
2.13 Vacation
2.20 Culture
2.26 Social Issue

Felipe *Colombia*
1.1 Introduction
1.7 Daily Routine
1.10 Childhood Memory
1.24 Culture
1.28 Social Issue

Jaime *Chile*
1.6 Introduction
1.15 Vacation
1.17 My Hometown
1.19 Culture
1.30 Social Issue

Florencia *Argentina*
2.6 Introduction
2.15 Vacation
2.18 My Hometown
2.24 Culture
2.30 Social Issue

Introduction

What is *Spanish Voices?*

Spanish Voices is a two-part series of short audio essays by contributors from around Latin America and Spain. Each speaker has provided a total of five audio essays, including a self-introduction, essays on cultural and social issues, as well as various personal topics such as vacations, childhood memories, their daily routines, and their hometowns. Each book features six speakers and 30 audio essay chapters, called *segments.* A segment consists of a transcription (text), English translation, as well as exercises designed to help you expand your vocabulary and improve your listening skills.

On **www.lingualism.com/sv1** you can:

- download or stream the accompanying audio tracks for **free**.
- practice the vocabulary and expressions with online interactive flashcards, quizzes, and games.

How is *Spanish Voices* different?

What makes *Spanish Voices* a unique and powerful learning tool is that the material is based on recordings of native speakers speaking naturally and off-the-cuff—*not* voice actors reading prepared scripts. You will hear the speakers occasionally make what you are sure are mistakes; and you're likely right. Words may be mispronounced or misused; grammatical rules may not always be followed; sentences may be left unfinished if the speaker decides to rephrase what they are saying. This poses an extra challenge for listening. However, it is also very insightful to hear natural, spoken Spanish at various speeds, in all its varieties, and by a range of native speakers. This is, unfortunately, something most coursebooks lack in favor of carefully prepared, unnaturally slow listenings in a neutral accent. **It is hoped that the *Spanish Voices* series fills this gap to provide some refreshingly natural, challenging opportunities for improving listening skills.**

Can I benefit from this book at my level of Spanish?

This book is best suited for intermediate and more advanced learners. However, even lower-level students can benefit from listening to and studying the segments. Just keep in mind that the goal is ***not*** to understand 100%. The first time you listen, depending on your level, you may understand, say, 1%, 10%, 50%, or 90% of what you hear in a segment. If, after going through the exercises and studying the text while relistening several times, you manage to increase the percentage you can understand, you will have made progress and are successfully developing your skills and pushing your level up. Taking this approach, the material in *Spanish Voices* can be useful to learners at a wide range of levels.

How to Use This Book

To get the most out of this book, you need to exercise a bit of **discipline**—discipline to resist reading the texts and their translations before you have thoroughly studied the listenings. This cannot be emphasized enough. Once you have read the texts and translations, the dynamics of what you can obtain from listening to the segments change fundamentally. You should first listen to a segment *several* times while working your way through the exercises. These have been designed to help you first understand the gist and gradually discover details as you relisten. Only once you have come to understand as much as you can through the exercises should you move on to study the text and translation that follow. This approach will result in maximum efficiency in improving your listening skills. A step-by-step guideline follows:

Guidelines

1. **CHOOSE A SEGMENT TO STUDY:** The segments can be studied in any order; however, there is somewhat of a gradual progression from shorter and slower segments to longer and faster segments through each book. The box to the right of the segment's title shows the speaker's name and country of origin, as well as the number of words in the audio essay and the rate of speech the speaker uses (words per minute). The MP3s that accompany *Spanish Voices* are available as free downloads at **www.lingualism.com/sv1**.

2. **TITLE AND KEY WORDS:** *Before you listen the first time, be sure to read the title of the segment and look over the "True or False" questions.* Going into a listening "blind"—without having any context, without even knowing the topic—makes listening comprehension in a foreign language extremely difficult. Just by knowing the general topic, we are able to improve the amount we can understand, as we are able to draw on knowledge from our past experiences, anticipate what might be said, recognize known words, and guess new words and phrases.

3. **TRUE OR FALSE:** *Answer the "True or False" questions.* (Do not read ahead to the multiple-choice questions as some of these questions themselves may answer the true-false questions.) If you feel unsure of your answers, listen to the audio again before checking your answers. You will notice that a small number follows most answers in the answer key. These numbers correspond to the line number in the text and translation that reveals the answer. If you do not understand *why* you got an answer wrong, quickly look at the text and/or translation for that line number. (Here's where you have to use your self-discipline *not* to read beyond the specified line number!) Listen again and place a check next to each *true or false* question as you hear the answer.

4. **EXPRESSIONS:** *Match the Spanish words and phrases to their English translations.* The vocabulary focuses mostly on high-frequency adverbs, connectors, and phrases. You will learn by spending time playing with the words, trying to match them up by process of elimination and educated guesses. So don't look up the answers too quickly! After you've matched the words and checked your answers, listen again while you check off the items as you hear them.

5. **MULTIPLE CHOICE:** *Answer the "Multiple Choice" questions.* Follow the same guidelines as for the *true or false* questions. Note that both the *true or false* and *multiple-choice* questions are based on

information found in the segment, according to the information provided by the speaker, regardless of the accuracy of the information. You can think of each question as being preceded by "According to *the speaker,* ..." or "*The speaker* mentions that...".

6. **TEXT AND TRANSLATION:** Now that you've worked your way through the first three exercises and have managed to pick up more of what has been said, you can feel free to move on to study the text and translation for the segment. This part is more *free-style.* Depending on your level of Spanish and level of comfort with the text, you can approach this in several ways. For instance, you can cover the Spanish side and first read the translation; then try to translate the English back into Spanish based on what you remember. Also, you can simply try to brainstorm some possible Spanish equivalents for the words or phrases in the English translation; then check the Spanish side and see how it was actually said. Conversely, you can cover the English side first and relisten while you read along with the Spanish, perhaps pausing the audio to repeat each line aloud. In any case, the side-by-side arrangement of the Spanish text and its English translation allows you to cover one side and test yourself in various ways. You should be able to match up most words and phrases with their equivalents in English. You may want to highlight useful and interesting vocabulary and phrases you want to learn.

7. **VOCABULARY:** Following the text and translation are two more exercises, which can be done while looking back at the text when needed. The "Vocabulary" exercise presents English translations for at least ten Spanish key words and phrases found in the segment. You can replay the audio while listening for the Spanish equivalents, and if needed, look back at the text. Each vocabulary item is followed by a reference to the line number where the Spanish word or phrase appears.

8. **TRANSLATE:** The "Translate" exercise requires two steps. First, you must circle the correct word(s) to complete each sentence. The purpose is to draw your attention to collocations and idioms and develop the very important skill of noticing *how* words are used together in sentences. The answer key shows the line number of the text where the structure in question can be found. The focus is on the little words—prepositions and pronouns, as well as verb forms such as the subjunctive. The second step is to translate the sentences into English. You will find suggested English translations in the answer key. Keep in mind that there is always more than one way to translate a sentence.

9. **LISTEN AGAIN:** Try listening to the segments you have already studied again later. You will find that you can understand more and with more ease the following day. (Studies have shown that material learned is consolidated and organized in the brain during sleep.)

The Texts and Translations

Lines

The text and translation for each segment have been divided into numbered "lines," which are not necessarily complete sentences or even clauses but are manageable chunks that can be studied.

Fillers

Fillers, which are used to signal that the speaker is thinking of what to say next, are a common and natural part of spoken language. Fillers vary from speaker and region. The most common and universal, are eh… and em…. Other popular fillers include bueno, este…, pues, entonces. Keep your ears open for such words and how native speakers use them. Another trait of spoken discourse is that the speaker may misspeak, then back up to correct themself. Also, a speaker may decide to rephrase a sentence or simply not finish it. These are all marked with ellipses (…) so that you can easily see that the *word* you didn't catch is, in fact, not a complete word at all. These ellipses are meant to aid you in deciphering the listening. However, when you are reading for meaning, anything before an ellipsis can be ignored.

The Translations

Good style has been sacrificed in favor of direct translations so that Spanish words and phrases can easily be matched up to their translations. You are encouraged to think of alternative ways lines could be translated into English.

Presentaciones

Felipe

Felipe (Colombia)
214 words (107 wpm)   ⊙1

True or False

1. Felipe lives alone in a small apartment in downtown Bogota.   T ☐ F ☐
2. He hopes to marry his current girlfriend someday.   T ☐ F ☐
3. He likes music, but he doesn't like dancing.   T ☐ F ☐
4. He speaks four languages.   T ☐ F ☐
5. His musical tastes are different from that of most people in his country.   T ☐ F ☐

Expressions

algún día	a bunch of
bueno	and the like
cerca de	anyway
como ya lo mencioné	as I mentioned
cosas por el estilo	everything that has to do with
de pronto*	I'd like to be able to
en fin	maybe
me gustaría poder	near
todo que tiene que ver con	someday
un montón de	things like that
y estas cosas	well, uh

Multiple Choice

1. Felipe lives with his mother, ___.

   a. brother, and nephew   c. brother, and niece
   b. sister, and niece   d. sister, and nephew

2. Felipe is a ___ and ___.

   a. musician   c. sound engineer
   b. scientist   d. linguist

3. Which of the follow does Felipe **not** mention he is interested in?

   a. traveling   c. movies
   b. sports   d. techno music

Text

¡Hola! ¿Qué tal?	1	Hey! How's it going?

Mi nombre es Felipe.	2	My name is Felipe.
Tengo treinta años.	3	I am 30 years old.
Soy de Bogotá, la capital de Colombia.	4	I am from Bogota, the capital of Colombia.
Vivo con mi mamá, mi hermana y mi sobrino.	5	I live with my mother, my sister, and my nephew.
Vivimos en Cogua, un pueblo cerca de Bogotá.	6	We live in Cogua, a small town near Bogota.
No soy casado pero tengo novia.	7	I am not married, but I have a girlfriend.
De pronto, nos casaremos algún día.	8*	Maybe someday we will get married.
Bueno, yo soy músico, productor de música, ingeniero de sonido.	9	Well, I am a musician, music producer, sound engineer.
Y bueno, me apasiona todo lo que tiene que ver con audio y estas cosas.	10	And well, I am passionate about everything related to audio and things like that.
Crecí en Bogotá; es una ciudad muy grande, muy chévere.	11	I grew up in Bogota; it is a very big city, and very cool.
Y bueno, me encanta viajar, conocer sitios nuevos, culturas, probar cosas nuevas.	12	And well, I love traveling, getting to know new places, cultures, trying new things.
También me encanta estudiar, aprender, todo lo que tiene que ver con lenguas... idiomas,	13	I also love studying, learning, everything about languages,
también ciencia, matemáticas, antropología, historia, psicología.	14	also, science, math, anthropology, history, psychology.
Bueno, en fin, un montón de cosas me interesan.	15	Well, anyway, a bunch of things interest me.
Eh... Hablo dos idiomas; estoy aprendiendo el tercero.	16	Uh... I speak two languages; I'm learning my third language now.
Me gustaría poder hablar muchos idiomas algún día.	17	I would like to be able to speak a lot of languages someday.
Em... En mi tiempo libre me gusta estar con mi novia,	18	Um... In my free time I like being with my girlfriend,
jugar con mi sobrino, ir a cine, ver películas, bailar, conversar, escuchar música, leer,	19	playing with my nephew, going to the cinema, watching movies, dancing, talking, listening to music, reading,
bueno, cosas por el estilo.	20	well, things like that.
¿Mi trabajo? Bueno, yo soy, como ya lo mencioné, músico,	21	My job? Well, as I mentioned, I am a musician,
y produzco música aquí en mi estudio.	22	and I produce music here in my studio.
Me gusta el house y el techno,	23	I like house and techno,
un poco diferente a lo que le gusta a la gente en este país,	24	[which is] a little different from what people in this country like,
pero bueno, es lo que me gusta.	25	but, well, it is what I like.
Bueno pues, ¡chao!	26	Alright, bye!

*8 To most Spanish speakers, *de pronto* means 'suddenly', but in Colombia it means 'maybe'.

Vocabulary

1. nephew[5]   _____
2. small town[6]   _____
3. to get married[8]   _____
4. engineer[9]   _____
5. to grow up[11]   _____

6. cool[11]   _____
7. to get to know[12]   _____
8. to try (out)[12]   _____
9. to mention[21]   _____
10. to produce[22]   _____

Translate

1. Juan vive en Oakland, una ciudad _cerca a / cerca de_ San Francisco.
2. _Casaron / Se casaron_ el año pasado
3. _Apasiono a / Me apasiona_ la poesía.
4. Me encanta _viajar / viajando_.
5. Soy _médico / un médico_.
6. Es _qué / lo que_ me gusta.

---

notes

(blank ruled note-taking space)

True or False: 1. F[6] 2. T[7-8] 3. F[18-19] 4. F[16] 5. T[23-25] **Expressions:** algún día - someday / Bueno – well, uh / cerca de - near / como ya lo mencioné - as I mentioned / cosas por el estilo - things like that / de pronto* - maybe / en fin - anyway / me gustaría poder - I'd like to be able to / todo que tiene que ver con - everything that has to do with / un montón de - a bunch of / y estas cosas - and the like **Multiple Choice:** 1. d[5] 2. a, c[9] 3. b **Vocabulary:** 1. sobrino 2. pueblo 3. casarse 4. ingeniero 5. crecer 6. chévere 7. conocer 8. probar 9. mencionar 10. producir **Translate:** 1. cerca de[6] Juan lives in Oakland, a city near San Francisco. 2. se casaron[8] They got married last year. 3. me apasiona[10] I'm passionate about poetry. 4. viajar[12] I love traveling. 5. médico[9] I'm a doctor. 6. lo que[25] That's what I like.

Melanie

Melanie (Mexico)
421 words (150 wpm)   ☉ 2

True or False

1. Melanie once moved to California for work.   T ☐ F ☐
2. She has a large family.   T ☐ F ☐
3. She enjoys her current job.   T ☐ F ☐
4. She thinks her hometown is pretty boring.   T ☐ F ☐
5. It takes Melanie nearly half an hour to climb up to the lighthouse (*el faro*).   T ☐ F ☐

Expressions

a finales de	alongside
a un lado de	another thing
apenas	at least
cada dos semanas	at the end of
este	barely, just
la mayor parte de	every other week
más de	I had to
me tuve que	less than
menos de	more than
otra cosa	most of
por lo menos	well, um

Multiple Choice

1. Melanie is currently ___ and ___.

   a. working as a teacher   c. studying to be an English teacher
   b. working at a hotel   d. studying hotel and tourism management

2. In her free time, Melanie enjoys ___ and ___.

   a. going to the beach   c. going camping with her cousins
   b. walking her dogs   d. skating along the boardwalk

3. How many aunts and uncles does Melanie have?

   a. 8   b. 10   c. 18   d. 40

Text

Hola, Soy Melanie. Tengo veintitrés años.	1	Hi, I'm Melanie. I'm 23 years old.
Soy mexicana y vivo en Mazatlán, Sinaloa.	2	I'm Mexican and I live in Mazatlan, Sinaloa.
He vivido aquí la mayor parte de mi vida.	3	I've lived here most of my life.
Solamente me he mudado en dos ocasiones.	4	I've moved only twice.
Una cuando tenía doce años, me fui a vivir con mi familia a California en Estados Unidos.	5	Once when I was 12 years old, I moved with my family to California, in the U.S.
Y la segunda vez que me mudé tenía dieciocho años y me mudé yo sola a Cozumel.	6	And the second time I moved I was 18 years old, and I moved by myself to Cozumel.

Fuí por parte del trabajo y ¡me encantó!	7	I went there for work, and I loved it!
Es una isla muy bonita aquí en México donde hay muchas cosas que hacer.	8	It is a very beautiful island here in Mexico where there is a lot to do.
Em... hay mucha naturaleza y ¡me encantó!	9	Um... there's a lot of nature and I loved it!
Pero me tuve que devolver a Mazatlán,	10	But I had to come back to Mazatlan,
porque extrañaba mucho a mi familia, a mis amigos,	11	because I really missed my family, my friends,
y quería estudiar una carrera.	12	and I wanted to earn a degree.
Ahorita estoy estudiando para ser maestra de inglés.	13	Right now I'm studying to be an English teacher.
Ya casi me gradúo este año, a finales de este año.	14	I'm about to graduate this year, at the end of the year.
y estoy trabajando en un hotel.	15	And I'm working at a hotel.
Me dediqué a ser maestra tres años,	16	I worked as a teacher for three years,
pero se me hizo muy pesado trabajar y estudiar.	17	but it was too hard to work and study.
Así es que decidí tomar un trabajo que fuera más... más sencillo y menos estresante.	18	So, I decided to take a job that was simpler... and less stressful.
Estoy muy contenta en el hotel.	19	I'm really happy at the hotel,
Tengo apenas como seis meses trabajando ahí y ¡me encanta!	20	I've just been working there, like, six months, and I love it!
Aquí en Mazatlán tengo mucha familia.	21	Here in Mazatlan I have a lot of family.
Tengo más de cuarenta primos.	22	I have more than 40 cousins.
Y mis papás tienen... mi papá tiene diez hermanos y mi mamá ocho.	23	And my parents... my dad has ten siblings and my mom eight.
Y todos somos muy unidos.	24	And we're all very close.
Nos encanta hacer reuniones familiares por lo menos cada dos semanas.	25	We love to have family gatherings at least every other week.
Y nos la pasamos muy bien.	26	And we have a really good time.
En Mazatlán hay muchas cosas que hacer.	27	There are many things to do in Mazatlan.
Lo que más me gusta hacer a mí es ir a la playa.	28	What I like doing most is going to the beach.
Me la paso súper bien.	29	I really enjoy it.
Me voy con mis amigos o con mis primos.	30	I go with my friends or cousins.
Llevo música, comida, este...	31	I bring music, food, um...
Nos metemos a la playa,	32	We go in the water,
nos encanta ver el atardecer,	33	We love watching the sun set,
o también me gusta ir a la alberca.	34	or I also like going to the pool.
Se nos pasa el día muy rápido y nos divertimos mucho.	35	The day goes by really fast, and we have a lot of fun.
Otra cosa que me gusta hacer aquí en Mazatlán es ir a patinar.	36	Something else I like to do here in Mazatlan is to go skating.
El malecón es muy grande, muy largo.	37	The boardwalk is very big and long.

Y... es muy relajante ir a patinar, ver a la gente.	38	And... it's really relaxing to go skating, watch people.
Mucha gente eh... acostumbra pasear a sus perros o caminar con sus hijos.	39	A lot of people uh... tend to walk their dogs or walk with their children.
Y es muy bonito patinar a un lado del mar escuchando las olas.	40	And it's really nice to skate alongside the sea while listening to the waves.
Otra cosa que me gusta hacer aquí en Mazatlán es subir el faro.	41	Another thing I like doing here in Mazatlan is to climb up the lighthouse.
El faro es... en Mazatlán tenemos el faro natural más grande del mundo.	42	The lighthouse is... in Mazatlan we have the world's highest natural lighthouse
Y lo puedo subir fácilmente en menos de diez minutos,	43	And I can easily go up in less than ten minutes,
y tengo una vista preciosa donde se ve toda la ciudad,	44	and have an amazing view where the whole city can be seen,
y el atardecer, si vas a esa hora, o a la hora del amanecer también se ve muy bonito.	45	and the sunset, if you go at that time, or at sunrise too it looks really pretty.

Vocabulary

1. to move[4] _____
2. to miss[11] _____
3. stressful[18] _____
4. close[24] _____
5. sunset[33] _____
6. pool[34] _____
7. to skate[36] _____
8. boardwalk[37] _____
9. relaxing[38] _____
10. to walk one's dog[39] _____
11. wave[40] _____
12. lighthouse[41] _____
13. sunrise[45] _____

Translate

1. Tengo muchas cosas *a hacer / que hacer*.
2. *Me hace / Se me hace* muy pesado dormir.
3. *Decidí / Me decidí* ir a patinar con mis amigos.
4. *Me la pasé / Me la pasó* muy bien anoche.
5. Mucha gente *acostumbra / se acostumbra* comer carne a diario.
6. Esta actriz es la mujer más hermosa *en el mundo / del mundo*.

notes

True or False: 1. F[5] 2. T[21-23] 3. T[19-20] 4. F[27] 5. F[43] **Expressions:** a finales de - at the end of / a un lado de - alongside / apenas - barely, just / cada dos semanas - every other week / este – well, um / la mayor parte de - most of / más de - more than / me tuve que - I had to / menos de - less than / otra cosa - another thing / por lo menos - at least **Multiple Choice:** 1. b[15], c[13] 2. a[28], d[36] 3. c[23] **Vocabulary:** 1. mudarse 2. extrañar 3. estresante 4. unido 5. atardecer 6. alberca 7. patina 8. malecón 9. relajante 10. pasear a su perro 11. ola 12. faro 13. amanecer **Translate:** 1. que hacer[8] I have a lot (of things) to do. 2. se me hace[17] It's really hard for me to sleep. 3. decidí[18] I decided to go skating with my friends. 4. me la pasé[26, 29] I had a great time last night. 5. acostumbra[39] A lot of people tend to eat meat on a daily basis. 6. del mundo[42] This actress is the most beautiful woman in the world.

Jared

Jared (Dominican Rep.)
332 words (104 wpm) ⊙ 3

True or False

1. Jared moved to Santo Domingo when he was 22 years old. T ☐ F ☐
2. He has never been outside of the Dominican Republic. T ☐ F ☐
3. He tells us a lot about his country. T ☐ F ☐
4. He is currently in college. T ☐ F ☐
5. He is interested in the performing arts. T ☐ F ☐

Expressions

como ya les dije	a little more
desde que	but
desde temprano	from an early age
etonces	I've been to
he ido a	like I said
lo que significa que	not exactly, not really
ningún otro sitio	not yet
no… que digamos	nowhere else
por ahí	really, actually
realmente	several years
sino que	since
todavía no	then, so, in that case
un poquito más	something like that
varios años	soon
y nada	well, anyway
ya pronto	which means that

Multiple Choice

1. Jared is studying ___.

    a. theater arts   b. advertising   c. *both a and b*   d. *neither a nor b*

2. Jared has been interested in singing, dancing, and acting ___.

    a. for five years   c. from an early age
    b. since he was 22 years old   d. since he took a performing arts class in college

3. Currently Jared is focused on ___.

    a. publishing his first book   c. earning money through his hobbies
    b. a career in musical theater   d. finishing college

Text

¿Qué tal? ¡Buen día! Mi nombre es Jared.	1	How are you? Good day! My name is Jared.
Tengo veintidós años y vivo en la República Dominicana.	2	I am 22 years old, and live in the Dominican Republic.

Eh... La ciudad en la que vivo se llama Santo Domingo.	3	Uh... The city where I live is called Santo Domingo.
Esa es la capital, y... nada.	4	That is the capital... and... anyway.
Yo vivo aquí desde pequeño.	5	I've lived here since I was little.
Realmente no he ido... no he viajado bastante que digamos.	6	I actually haven't really gone... I haven't exactly traveled much.
He viajado un poco—he ido a Puerto Rico, he ido a Panamá, he ido a Venezuela, a Colombia...	7	I've traveled a bit—I've been to Puerto Rico, I've been to Panama, I've been to Venezuela, Colombia...
Pero realmente me he quedado aquí en mi país.	8	But really I've stayed here in my country.
No he... no he viaja-... no he ... no me he mudado para ningún otro sitio.	9	I haven't... I haven't trav-... I haven't... I haven't moved anywhere else.
Vivo en el mismo sitio que nací.	10	I live in the same place I was born.
Eh... ¿Qué les digo sobre... sobre mi país?	11	Uh... What should I tell you about... about my country?
Bueno, no voy a hablar tanto de mi país todavía; voy a hablar un poquito más sobre mí.	12	Well, I won't talk much about my country yet; I'll talk a little more about myself.
Como ya les dije tengo veintidós años y vivo aquí en República Dominicana,	13	As I've already mentioned, I am 22 years old, and I live here in the Dominican Republic,
lo que significa que ya debería estar en la universidad.	14	which means that I should already be in college.
Y sí, estoy en la universidad, acabando, realmente.	15	And I am in college, finishing up, actually.
Eh... estoy estudiando publicidad... y... ya estoy en la tesis,	16	Uh... I'm studying advertising... and... I'm already doing my thesis,
lo que significa que ya pronto podré trabajar.	17	which means that I'll be able to work soon.
Todavía no he comenzado a trabajar sino que para ganar dinero me dedico... un poquito a...	18	I haven't started to work yet, but to earn money I work as... a little...
bueno, para ganar dinero me dedico un poquito a mis hobbies, que son realmente, cantar, bailar y actuar.	19	well, to earn a money I work a bit with my hobbies, which are actually singing, dancing, and acting.
Tengo cantando, bailando y actuando desde que tengo... m-... memoria casi—muy muy temprano.	20	I've been singing, dancing, and acting almost as far back as I can... re-... remember—very, very early.
Desde los cinco años ya yo decía que yo iba a bailar y a cantar... y bueno a actuar.	21	From age five, I was already saying that I was going to dance and sing... and, well, to act.
Y realmente eh... comencé... comencé a tomar clases,	22	And really, uh... I started... started to take lessons
eh... desde temprano tomé varios años de teatro, tomé varios años de baile y... y canté, por ahí.	23	uh... from an early age I took several years of theater, took several years of dancing and... I sang, something like that.
Em... y realmente, me ha funcionado.	24	Um... and really, it's worked for me.
Yo... no te puedo decir que... que vivo de esto, pero... sí que pudiera si me lo propusiera.	25	I... I can't tell you that... that I'm making a living off this, but... I could if I put my mind to it.

Realmente 'toy... estoy enfocado en... en terminar la universidad.	26	Really, I'm... I'm focused on... on finishing college.
Y luego, voy a decidir si me quiero quedar haciendo teatro musical, o si... me quedaré haciendo publicidad.	27	And then I'll decide if I want to keep doing musical theater, or if... I'll keep doing advertising.
Realmente, las dos cosas me apasionan. Las dos me gustan.	28	Actually, I'm passionate about both. I like both.
Entonces na'... eso es lo que yo puedo decir de mí.	29	So... anyway, that is what I can say about myself.

Vocabulary

1. to stay[8]
2. to be born[10]
3. to finish[15]
4. actually[15]
5. to work in, make a living from[19]

6. thesis[16]
7. to act[19]
8. advertising[16]
9. to take a class[22]
10. to put one's mind to[25]

Translate

1. ¿Qué *las / les* digo sobre mí?
2. Quiero comenzar *a / de* meditar.
3. Parece que no *lo funcionas / te funciona* muy bien.
4. Pudiera vivir de mi hobby si me lo *propusiera / proponga*.
5. Me quedé *a hacer / haciendo* lo que amo.
6. Quiero hablar un poquito sobre *mí / mi*.

notes

True or False: 1. F[3-5] 2. F[7] 3. F[12] 4. T[15] 5. T[19] **Expressions:** como ya les dije - like I said / desde que - since / desde temprano - from an early age / entonces – then, so, in that case / he ido a - I've been to / lo que significa que - which means that / ningún otro sitio - nowhere else / no... que digamos - not exactly, not really / realmente - really, actually / sino que - but / todavía no - not yet / un poquito más - a little more / varios años - several years / y nada - well, anyway / ya pronto - soon **Multiple Choice:** 1. b[16] 2. c[21-23] 3. d[26] **Vocabulary:** 1. quedarse 2. nacer 3. acabar 4. realmente 5. dedicarse a 6. tesis 7. actuar 8. publicidad 9. tomar una clase 10. proponerse **Translate:** 1. les[11] What can I tell you about myself? 2. a[22] I want to start meditating. 3. te funciona[24] It doesn't look like it's working (out) for you very well. 4. propusiera[25] I could live off (*or* make a living from) my hobby if I put my mind to it. 5. haciendo[27] I kept (on) doing what I love. 6. mí[12] I want to talk a bit about myself.

Chelo

Chelo (Spain)
369 words (175 wpm) ⊙ 4

True or False

1. Chelo lives with her parents in a house in the suburbs of Valencia.   T ☐ F ☐
2. She is an only child.   T ☐ F ☐
3. She is studying translation and interpretation at a university in Madrid.   T ☐ F ☐
4. Her dream is to work at the United Nations.   T ☐ F ☐
5. She mentions what she enjoys doing with her friends.   T ☐ F ☐

Expressions

actualmente	after all
además de	all kinds of __
al fin y al cabo	although
así que	currently, at present
aunque	however
__ de todo tipo	I mean
me refiero	I'm passionate about
sin embargo	in addition to
soy un apasionado de	not yet
todavía no	so, therefore

Multiple Choice

1. Chelo can speak __ and __.

   a. Polish   c. German
   b. Valencian   d. Italian

2. Which of the following is **not** true about Chelo?

   a. She is close to her cousins, who also live in Valencia.
   b. She works at a translation agency in Valencia.
   c. She does not regret the major she chose at university.
   d. She is thinking about moving in with her boyfriend.

3. Chelo thinks she can learn Portuguese quickly because ___.

   a. it is quite similar to Spanish
   b. her boyfriend is Portuguese
   c. she is planning to move to Portugal
   d. she is really good at learning languages

Text

¡Hola! Soy Chelo y tengo veinticuatro años.	1	Hey! I am Chelo, and I am 24 years old.
Nací en Valencia, ciudad en la que vivo actualmente.	2	I was born in Valencia, the city where I currently live in.
Valencia es una ciudad al este de España, cerca del mar Mediterráneo.	3	Valencia is a city located in the East of Spain, close to the Mediterranean sea.
Vivo con mis padres en el centro de la ciudad en un piso,	4	I live with my parents in an apartment downtown,

como todas las personas que viven en el centro de Valencia,	5	as do all people who live in the center of Valencia,
porque aquí no suele haber casas.	6	because there tend not to be any houses here.
Em... Soy hija única, aunque nunca he echado de menos tener ningún hermano:	7	Um... I am an only child, although I have never missed having a sibling:
tengo una relación muy cercana con mis primos,	8	I have a close relationship with my cousins,
así que... nunca he echado de menos tener ningún hermano o hermana,	9	so... I have never missed having a brother or sister,
porque viven en la misma ciudad que yo, me refiero.	10	because they live in the same city as me, I mean.
Estudié el bachillerato de humanidades,	11*	In high school I specialized in humanities,
y dos años después empecé la carrera de traducción e interpretación en Valencia también.	12	and two years later, I started studying a translation and interpretation degree also in Valencia.
¡Creo que nunca me arrepentiré de haber escogido este grado en la universidad!	13	I don't think I'll ever regret my choice of studies at university!
¡Porque es una carrera que me encanta y que disfruto muchísimo!	14	Because it's a field I love and really enjoy!
Como podréis imaginar, soy una apasionada de los idiomas.	15	As you can see, I'm passionate about languages.
Em... Además de español y valenciano, la lengua de donde vivo, hablo inglés, francés y alemán.	16*	Um... in addition to Spanish and Valencian, the language from where I live, I can also speak English, French, and German.
Estudio portugués desde hace un año.	17	I've been studying Portuguese for a year.
Y... creo que pronto tendré un buen nivel porque se parece mucho al español,	18	And... I think I'll be at a good level soon because it's quite similar to Spanish,
así que es bastante sencillo para mí.	19	so it isn't difficult for me.
También me gustaría aprender polaco,	20	I'd also like to learn Polish,
aunque todavía no me he decidido.	21	but I haven't decided it yet.
Cuando terminé la universidad, empecé a trabajar como traductora autónoma.	22	When I finished college, I started working as a freelance translator.
Es un trabajo que me encanta porque traduzco desde varios idiomas y culturas y...	23	It's a job I love because I translate from various languages and cultures and...
Al fin y al cabo, es lo que he estudiado en la universidad y lo que más me gusta.	24	After all, it is what I studied at university and what I like the most.
Traduzco textos de todo tipo, así que siempre aprendo algo nuevo,	25	I translate texts of all kinds so I always learn something new,
aunque también tengo temas en los que más me gusta trabajar como, por ejemplo, la cultura, el intercambio cultural, los viajes o el comercio on-line.	26	although there are also topics I like working with the best, for example, culture, culture exchange, travel, and e-commerce.
Sin embargo, mi verdadero sueño sería llegar a ser intérprete de la ONU;	27	However, my real dream is to become an interpreter at the U.N.;
aunque tendría que trabajar muchísimo para llegar a conseguir ese puesto.	28	although I'd have to work a lot to get that position.

Así que sigo esforzándome cada día por conseguir mi sueño.	29	For that reason, I always do my best in order to achieve my dream.	
En mi tiempo libre, me gusta ir a la playa con mis amigas o ir de compras y sentarnos en algún café a charlar y pasar la tarde.	30	In my free time, I like going to the beach with my friends, or going shopping and sitting a café to chat and spend the afternoon.	
Últimamente también me dedico mi tiempo a leer revistas de decoración,	31	Lately, I also spend my free time reading magazines about home decor,	
porque mi novio y yo estamos pensando en irnos a vivir juntos.	32	because my boyfriend and I are thinking about moving in together.	

*11 The Spanish baccalaureate (*bachillerato*) is a two-year track at the end of secondary education, similar to A Levels in the U.K. As a preparatory program for university, students specialize in one of four branches: arts, science and technology, social sciences, or humanities.

*16 Valencian is a variety of Catalan, a Romance language spoken in northeastern Spain. In the region, it is co-official with Spanish.

Vocabulary

1. apartment[4] _____
2. only child[7] _____
3. to miss[9] _____
4. baccalaureate[11] _____
5. major, degree[12] _____
6. level[18] _____
7. Polish[20] _____
8. freelance[22] _____

9. to become[27] _____
10. interpreter[27] _____
11. the U.N.[27] _____
12. position (job)[28] _____
13. to go shopping[30] _____
14. to chat[30] _____
15. to do one's best (in order) to[29] _____

Translate

1. Málaga es una ciudad *en España del sur / al sur de España*.
2. Suele *haber / que haya* muchos coches en esta carretera.
3. *Echo / Me echa* de menos mi infancia.
4. Alberto se arrepiente *por / de* haber hecho eso.
5. Teresa trabaja aquí *desde hace / hace desde* seis meses.
6. Seguiré *esforzándome por / a esforzarme para* encontrar un empleo.

*** notes ***

_____

True or False: 1. F[4] 2. T[7] 3. F[12] 4. T[27] 5. T[30] **Expressions:** actualmente - currently, at present / además de - in addition to / al fin y al cabo - after all / así que - so, therefore / aunque - although / __ de todo tipo - all kinds of __ / me refiero - I mean / sin embargo - however / soy un apasionado de - I'm passionate about / todavía no - not yet **Multiple Choice:** 1. b, c[16] 2. b[8-10, 22, 13, 32] 3. a[18-19] **Vocabulary:** 1. piso 2. hijo único 3. echar de menos 4. bachillerato 5. carrera 6. nivel 7. polaco 8. autónomo 9. llegar a ser 10. intérprete 11. la ONU 12. puesto 13. ir de compras 14. charlar 15. esforzarse por **Translate:** 1. al sur de España[3] Malaga is a city in the south of Spain (*or* in southern Spain). 2. haber[6] There are usually a lot of cars on this road. 3. echo[7] I miss my childhood. 4. de[13] Alberto regrets having done that. 5. desde hace[17] Teresa has been working here for six months. 6. esforzándome por[29] I'll keep doing my best to find a job.

Gisela

Gisela (Venezuela)
165 words (108 wpm) ⊙5

True or False

1. Gisela was born in Maracaibo. T ☐ F ☐
2. She is married. T ☐ F ☐
3. She has a degree in English literature. T ☐ F ☐
4. She can speak English very well. T ☐ F ☐
5. She has a lot of free time to pursue her hobbies. T ☐ F ☐

Expressions

actualmente	currently, at present
así que	due to
de vez en cuando	for many years
en vista de que	I had to
fundamentalmente	little by little
hasta que	mainly
poco a poco	once in a while
por	since, in light of
por muchos años	so, therefore
pues	so, well
tuve que	until

Multiple Choice

1. Gisela has ___.

   a. six children
   b. four sons and one daughter
   c. two sons
   d. two daughters

2. Gisela currently works ___.

   a. as a translator
   b. as an organizational specialist
   c. in a psychiatric hospital
   d. in England

3. Which of the following does Gisela enjoy doing in her free time?

   a. jigsaw puzzles
   b. people watching
   c. reading
   d. *all of the above*

Text

¡Hola! ¿cómo estás? Me llamo Gisela.	1	Hi! How are you? My name is Gisela.
Nací en Venezuela en la ciudad de Maracaibo, en el estado Zulia.	2	I was born in Venezuela in the city of Maracaibo, in the state of Zulia.
Em... Pero mis padres se mudaron a Caracas cuando yo estaba muy pequeña.	3	Um... but my parents moved to Caracas when I was very small.
Así que me crié en Caracas realmente, que es la capital de... del país, de Venezuela.	4	So I actually grew up in Caracas, which is the capital of the country, of Venezuela.

Eh... Soy la cuarta de seis hermanos; tengo cuatro hermanos y una hermana.	5	Uh... I'm the fourth of six siblings; I have four brothers and one sister.
Eh... Soy divorciada; tengo dos hijos, maravillosos hijos.	6*	Uh... I'm divorced, and have two sons, wonderful sons.
Em... Estudié psicología en Caracas y me gradué de psicólogo.	7	Um... I studied psychology in Caracas and graduated as a psychologist.
Tengo un titulo como psicólogo.	8	I have a psychology degree.
Por muchos años trabajé ejerciendo mi profesión, eh... como especialista en desarrollo organizacional, diseñando pues y dictando cursos de adiestramiento para las empresas.	9	For many years I worked practicing my profession, uh... as an organizational development specialist, so [I was] designing and giving training courses for companies.
Y bueno, por la situación difícil sucedida en el país, en Venezuela, eh... tuve que buscar hacer otras cosas.	10	And well, due to the difficult situation that occurred in the country, in Venezuela, uh... I had to look for other things to do.
Y bueno, en vista de que... eh... yo sé inglés— sé hablar inglés, conozco el idioma inglés muy bien—	11	And well, since I... uh... know English—I speak English and know the English language very well—
pues entonces decidí ofrecer mis servicios... eh... traduciendo, como traductora inglés-español.	12	so I decided to offer my services... uh... translating, as an English-Spanish translator.
Y eso es lo que hago actualmente.	13	And that is what I currently do.
Eh... vengo trabajando haciendo proyectos de traducción inglés-español eh... por Internet.	14	Uh... I've been working doing English-Spanish translation projects... uh... on the Internet.
Eso es eh... lo que hago como trabajo fundamentalmente.	15	That is uh... what I mainly do for work.
Entre las cosas que me gusta hacer en mi tiempo libre, cuando tengo tiempo libre porque normalmente, realmente no tengo... no tengo tiempo libre, eh... trabajo bastante.	16	Among the things I like to do in my free time, when I have free time, because usually, I really don't have any... I don't have free time, uh... I work a lot.
Pero me... me gusta mucho leer.	17	But I... I really like to read.
Em... me encanta hacer rompecabezas.	18	Um... I love to do jigsaw puzzles.
Entonces pues... comienzo un rompecabezas y... y lo dejo y trabajo con él poco a poco hasta que lo termino.	19	So, well... I start building up a puzzle and... and I put it aside and work on it little by little until I complete it.
Me encanta salir a pasear, sencillamente ir a caminar, pararme en un lugar, sentarme a observar a la gente caminando, observar lo que hacen.	20	I love to go out for walks, simply to go walking, stop somewhere, sit down and watch people walking, observe what they do...
Em... y bueno, en general me gusta también mucho compartir, compartir con mis hijos eh... conversar, conversar con ellos, y también de vez en cuando conversar eh... con mis amigas, con mis amistades.	21	Um... and well, in general I very much like to share, share with my sons uh... talk with them and also once in a while talk uh... with my girlfriends, with my friends.

*6 You can say *ser* or *estar* with words like *casado* and *divorciado*.

Vocabulary

1. to move to[3] _____
2. to grow up in[4] _____
3. wonderful[6] _____
4. degree, diploma[8] _____
5. psychologist[8] _____
6. development[9] _____

7. training[9] _____
8. company[9] _____
9. puzzle[18] _____
10. to share with[21] _____
11. friends[21] _____
12. to go out for a walk[20] _____

Translate

1. Carlota trabajó en esa empresa *para / por* muchos años.
2. No lo veo mucho, en vista *porque / de que* trabaja en otro departamento ahora.
3. Yo *sé / conozco* hablar francés.
4. Javier se sentó *para / a* leer la carta.
5. *Me encanta / Encanto* salir a pasear.
6. Cuando me pongo a trabajar en algo, no paro hasta *lo que / que lo* termino.

---

notes

Jaime

Jaime (Chile)
468 words (199 wpm)   💿 6

True or False

1. Jaime lives with his girlfriend.   T ☐ F ☐
2. He loves music, especially playing the guitar.   T ☐ F ☐
3. He considers himself to be quite good at sports.   T ☐ F ☐
4. He considers himself to be quite extroverted and has lots of friends.   T ☐ F ☐
5. He lives in a small city about two hours from the capital, Santiago.   T ☐ F ☐

Expressions

aún	
como recién dije	_ ago
desafortunadamente	after that
desde chico	all my life
después	and then
durante	as for
el próximo año	as I just said
en cuanto a	for (time)
en este último tiempo	however
en ocasiones	in general
hace _	moreover
muy seguido	next year
por lo general	often
por lo tanto	rarely
por otra parte	recently, lately (x3)
principalmente	since I was little
quién sabe	sometimes
rara vez	still
recién	therefore
sin embargo	to have in mind
tener en mente	unfortunately
toda la vida	usually, mostly
últimamente	who knows
y luego	

Multiple Choice

1. Put the following four events in order.

   a. Jaime finished his studies.   c. Jaime studied to be a sound technician.
   b. Jaime worked at a radio station.   d. Jaime started playing the guitar.

2. In the future, Jaime wants to ___ and ___.

   a. move to Santiago   c. release a rock album
   b. live together with his girlfriend d. take over his parent's winery

3. Which of the following does Jaime **not** say about his hometown.

    a. It is located near the mountains.
    b. It is quite noisy and polluted.
    c. He has lived there all his life.
    d. It is quiet and not very entertaining.

Text

¡Hola! Mi nombre es Jaime y soy de Chile.	1	Hello! My name is Jaime and I'm from Chile.
Tengo veinticinco años, y vivo en la ciudad de San Fernando.	2	I'm 25 years old, and I live in San Fernando.
Tengo dos hermanas y un hermano.	3	I have two sisters and one brother.
Y actualmente me encuentro pololeando.	4	and currently I have a girlfriend.
Sólo he pololeado una vez, y ya llevamos casi seis años juntos.	5	I've only ever had one girlfriend, and we've been together for almost six years.
Desafortunadamente, aún vivimos con nuestros padres,	6	Unfortunately, we still live with our parents,
pero ya estamos planeando ir a vivir juntos el próximo año.	7	but we're planning to live together next year.
En cuanto a mis estudios, yo he estudiado dos carreras.	8	As for my studies, I've had two majors.
La primera fue técnico en sonido que fue dos años y medio,	9	The first one was sound technician for two years and a half,
y luego traducción en inglés durante cuatro años.	10	and then English translation for four years.
Trabajé en una radio muy conocida de Chile,	11	I worked at a very well-known radio station in Chile,
pero después me di cuenta que eso no era lo mío, lo que me gustaba.	12	but after that I realized that it wasn't for me, [wasn't] what I wanted.
Así que por lo tanto, decidí estudiar inglés que era lo que me apasionaba desde chico.	13	Therefore, I decided to study English, something I've really loved ever since I was little.
Terminé mi carrera de traducción hace unos meses,	14	I completed my studies in translation a couple of months ago,
así que estoy recién empezando a realizar traducciones para diferentes empresas,	15	so I'm just starting to translate for different companies,
con eso me ha alcanzado para vivir en este último tiempo.	16	which has been enough for me to live on lately.
El principal pasatiempos en mi vida es la música, particularmente la guitarra.	17	My favorite hobby in my life is music, particularly guitar.
Toco hace ya más de diez años.	18	I've been playing for more than ten years.
Y mis principales influencias son el rock de los setenta y noventa.	19	And my major influences are rock from the 70s and 90s.
Por lo general, no me gusta aprender canciones de otros artistas.	20	In general, I don't like learning songs from other artists.
Prefiero componer mis propias canciones.	21	I prefer to compose my own songs.
Tengo muchas ideas en mente,	22	I have many ideas in mind,
así que quién sabe, algún día pretendo lanzar mi primer disco de rock.	23	so who knows, one day I aspire to release my first rock album.

En mis tiempos libres como recién dije, me encanta tocar guitarra,	24	In my free time, as I just said, I love playing the guitar,
así que eso es lo que hago principalmente.	25	so that's what I usually do.
Aunque no soy muy bueno para los deportes, últimamente estoy yendo al gimnasio.	26	Even though I'm not very good at sports, I've been going to the gym lately.
También en ocasiones salgo con mi polola a bailar, vamos a comer.	27	Also, I sometimes go out dancing with my girlfriend, we eat out.
También vamos muy seguido a la playa que queda a unas dos horas de acá,	28	Also, we often go to the beach that it is two hours away from here,
para desconectarnos un poco de la ciudad, del ruido, y desestresarnos un poco.	29	to forget the city a bit, the noise, and to reduce stress a little.
En cuanto a mi personalidad, me considero una persona tranquila, introvertida.	30	As for my personality, I consider myself a quiet person, introverted.
Soy de pocos amigos.	31	I have few friends.
Pero, sin embargo, soy bastante alegre y tengo muy buen sentido del humor.	32	But, however, I'm very cheerful and have a very good sense of humor.
Yo soy nacido y criado en San Fernando.	33	I was born and raised in San Fernando.
Toda la vida la he vivido en esta parte.	34	All my life I've lived here.
San Fernando es una ciudad pequeña y es una mezcla de campo y ciudad.	35	San Fernando is a small city and is a mix of countryside and city.
Se encuentra más o menos cerca de la cordillera,	36	It is located near the mountain range,
y esta zona se destaca por su producción de vinos.	37	and this area is known for its wine production.
San Fernando se encuentra a dos horas de Santiago, que es la capital de Chile.	38	San Fernando is two hours away from Santiago, the capital of Chile.
Por lo general, a la gente de región no le gusta mucho la capital,	39	Generally, people from [this] region don't like the capital,
ya que es muy ruidosa, hay mucho estrés, hay mucha más contaminación, las calles llenas, el metro colapsado.	40	because it is very noisy, stressful, and there's a lot of pollution, streets are overcrowded, the metro is collapsed.
Así que aunque sea una ciudad pequeña y no muy entretenida, no la cambiamos por Santiago.	41	So even though it is a small city and not very fun, we wouldn't trade it for Santiago.
Por otra parte, esta zona es más tranquila, limpia, y hay menores niveles de delincuencia.	42	Moreover, this area is quieter, cleaner, and levels of crime are lower.
Podemos respirar aire puro.	43	We can breathe pure air.
Podemos ver las estrellas, que en Santiago rara vez es posible ver.	44	We can see the stars, which you can rarely see in Santiago.

Vocabulary

1. to be dating[4] _____
2. major (of study)[8] _____
3. well known[11] _____
4. to do, carry out[15] _____
5. to be enough[16] _____
6. to intend to[23] _____
7. to launch, release[23] _____
8. to play the guitar[24] _____
9. girlfriend[27] _____
10. to forget about one's worries[29] _____
11. to de-stress, relax[29] _____
12. mountain range[36] _____
13. to be known for[37] _____
14. noisy[40] _____
15. stress[40] _____
16. pollution[40] _____
17. collapsed[40] _____
18. entertaining, fun[41] _____
19. crime[42] _____
20. to have a good sense of humor[32] _____

Translate

1. *Estamos / Llevamos* cinco meses juntos.
2. Planeo *aprender / a aprender* a tocar guitarra.
3. Duró *dos horas y media / dos y media horas*.
4. *Victor tiene / es* de pocos amigos.
5. Me gradué *desde hace / hace* un año.
6. *Apasionaba a / Le apasionaba* la vida.

---

notes

Rutinas Diarias

La Rutina Diaria de Felipe

Felipe (Colombia)
353 words (152 wpm) 💿 7

True or False

1. Felipe is early to bed and early to rise.   T ☐ F ☐
2. He goes to the gym every morning.   T ☐ F ☐
3. He eats breakfast with his nephew.   T ☐ F ☐
4. He works from home.   T ☐ F ☐
5. He is learning some foreign languages.   T ☐ F ☐

Expressions

a esa hora	a couple of
a las _ en punto	and anyway
en subida	and then
más o menos	at _ o'clock sharp
me pongo a	at that time
me toca	I have to
por eso	I start to
sin falta	more or less
un par de	that's why
y luego	uphill
y nada	without exception

Multiple Choice

1. Who usually gets Felipe's nephew ready for school?

   a. Felipe's mother   c. Felipe
   b. Felipe's sister   d. Felipe's nephew gets ready by himself.

2. Which of the following <u>two</u> are **not** part of Felipe's daily routine?

   a. picking up his sister from work   c. making music
   b. reading the news   d. taking a nap

3. Before going to sleep, Felipe likes to ___.

   a. watch TV   b. read   c. check his email   d. exercise

Text

¿Mi rutina diaria?	1	My daily routine?
Bueno, los días son diferentes, pero algunas cosas siempre son fijas.	2	Well, the days are different but some things are always fixed.
Y bueno, tienen horarios estipulados.	3	And, well, they have schedules set out.

Por eso en días sin eventualidades, las cosas son algo así:	4	That's why, on uneventful days, things go something like this:
Primero me despierto entre las cuatro y media y las cinco de la mañana.	5	First, I wake up between a half past 4 and 5 a.m.
Y lo primero que hago es:	6	And the first thing I do is:
me levanto, me pongo la ropa para hacer deporte y voy al parque.	7	I get up, put on sports clothes, and go to the park.
Hago ejercicio como quince - veinte minutos o media hora.	8	I work out for like 15 or 20 minutes or half an hour.
Luego de hacer ejercicio, llego a la casa, me baño, me visto y me alisto.	9	After working out, I get home, take a shower, get dressed and get ready.
Y tengo que preparar el desayuno para mi sobrino,	10	And I have to make breakfast for my nephew,
pues a esa hora ya se ha ido mi mamá y mi hermana—	11	because at that time my sister and my mother have already left—
ya se han ido al trabajo y queda el niño aquí conmigo.	12	they have already left for work, and the boy [is] here with me.
Entonces me toca darle desayuno, alistarlo para ir al colegio y luego llevarlo al colegio.	13	So, I have to give him breakfast, get him ready for school, and then take him to school.
Lo bueno es que el colegio queda como a unas cinco cuadras de aquí.	14	What's nice is that the school is, like, about five blocks from here.
Entonces pues solo voy caminando.	15	So, I just walk there.
Eso si, es en subida—me toca subir una colina.	16	Of course, it's uphill—I have to go up a hill.
Lo dejo en el colegio; regreso a la casa.	17	I drop him at school and come back home.
Y entonces pues, hago desayuno, desayuno y nada.	18	And then I make breakfast, eat breakfast, and anyway.
Me siento en mi oficina a revisar correos,	19	I sit in my office and read emails,
veo noticias, leo las noticias, lo que ha pasado.	20	look at the news, read the news, what has happened.
Y luego me pongo a trabajar.	21	And then I get to work.
Entonces me pongo a hacer música,	22	So, I start making music,
o si no son… si no es música, son cosas relacionadas con la música	23	or if they're not… if it isn't music, it's music-related stuff,
como ya saben, diseño, management y vainas así.	24	like, you know, design or management, stuff like that.
Em… A las doce, más o menos a las doce, pongo a hacer el almuerzo,	25	Um… At noon, more or less at noon, I make lunch,
porque a las doce y media tengo que ir a recoger a mi sobrino.	26	because at half past twelve I have to go and pick up my nephew.
Entonces lo recojo y luego cuando llegamos acá almorzamos.	27	So, I pick him up, and then when we get here we have lunch.
Luego trabajo un poco más.	28	Then I work some more.
Luego hacemos tareas,	29	Then we do [his] homework,
y a eso de las cuatro de la tarde, dejo de trabajar.	30	and around four in the afternoon, I stop working.
Y me pongo a estudiar: estudio idiomas.	31	And I begin studying: I study languages.

Luego a las cinco en punto sin falta tengo que comer la cena,	32	Then at five o'clock without exception I have to eat dinner,	
y a las seis de la tarde me acuesto y leo un par de horas por ahí hasta las ocho de la noche.	33	and at six in the evening I go to bed and read for a couple of hours until maybe 8 p.m.	
Y luego apago todo ¡y a dormir!	34	And then I turn everything off and off to sleep!	
y ya, ¡hasta mañana! Es un día más o menos normal. ¡chao!	35	And that's it, until the next day! That's a normal day, more or less. Bye!	

Vocabulary

1. fixed, set[2] _____
2. stipulated, set out[3] _____
3. uneventful[4] _____
4. to get dressed[9] _____
5. to get ready[9] _____
6. nephew[10] _____
7. (city) block[14] _____
8. to check email[19] _____
9. thing[24] _____
10. to pick up, go get[26] _____
11. to go to bed[33] _____
12. to turn off[34] _____

Translate

1. Luego *cenando / de cenar*, me acuesto.
2. Le toca *hacer / de hacer* sus tareas cada día.
3. *Lo / Le* llevo a la escuela cada mañana.
4. Me senté *a / para* leer las noticias.
5. Dejé *a / de* estudiar hace una hora.
6. Se acuesta a las once *en / de* punto.

notes

La Rutina Diaria de Melanie

True or False

1. Melanie is usually the first person in her house to get up in the morning.   T ☐ F ☐
2. She has breakfast and then leaves the house around 7:30 a.m.   T ☐ F ☐
3. She goes to the gym after work with a friend.   T ☐ F ☐
4. She usually runs errands on Saturday afternoons.   T ☐ F ☐
5. She works five days a week.   T ☐ F ☐

Expressions

a veces	a little later
antes de	also, as well
así es que	at night
de la noche	before
de la tarde	either, neither
lo más temprano que	I have to
más o menos	in order to
para	in the afternoon
también	more or less, around
tampoco	so, therefore
tengo que	sometimes
un poco más tarde	the earliest that

Multiple Choice

1. Put the following four events in order.

   a. She goes to work.   c. She goes to the gym.
   b. She has dinner.   d. She goes to school.

2. Melanie gets off work on Saturdays at ___ and Sundays at ___.

   a. 12 or 1 p.m.   c. 2 or 3 p.m.
   b. 1 or 2 p.m.   d. 5 p.m.

3. Which of the following does Melanie **not** mention doing on Fridays?

   a. sleeping in a little   c. doing housework
   b. running errands   d. doing homework

Text

Normalmente me levanto a las seis de la mañana.	1	Usually I get up at 6 in the morning.
Eh… soy la primera en mi casa en despertarse.	2	Uh… I'm the first one in my house to wake up.
Así es que intento no hacer mucho ruido.	3	So, I try not to make a lot of noise.
Me gusta bañarme temprano para irme fresca al trabajo.	4	I like taking showers early in the morning to go to work feeling fresh.

Me maquillo, me peino, me cambio.	5	I do my make-up, my hair, get dressed.
Y hago mi maleta para irme al gimnasio después del trabajo.	6	And I prepare my bag to go to the gym after work.
A las siete y media salgo de mi casa.	7	At 7:30 I leave home.
Y paso por mi compañera,	8	And I go by my colleague's,
la recojo en su casa,	9	I pick her up from her house,
y nos vamos al trabajo.	10	and we go to work.
Entramos a las ocho y allá desayunamos.	11	We start at eight and have breakfast there.
No tenemos una hora específica de salida,	12	We don't have a specific time we get off work
pero... lo más temprano que ponemos salir es a las doce del mediodía.	13	but... the earliest we can leave is at twelve noon.
Lo que normalmente salimos es una o dos de la tarde,	14	It's usually 1 or 2 p.m. when we get off,
y lo más tarde que nos hemos quedado es a las cinco de la tarde.	15	and the latest we have stayed is until 5 p.m.
Después del trabajo, mi compañera y yo nos vamos al gimnasio.	16	After work, my colleague and I go to the gym.
Nos vamos dos horas o dos horas y media.	17	We go for two or two and a half hours.
Y después, cada quien se va a su casa,	18	and then everyone goes home,
comemos, nos bañamos y nos arreglamos para irnos a la escuela.	19	we eat, shower and get ready to go to school.
A veces, cuando tengo mucha tarea, no voy al gimnasio.	20	Sometimes when I have a lot of homework, I don't go to the gym.
Y me vengo a mi casa para hacer tarea antes de irme a la escuela.	21	And I come home to do homework before going to school.
A la escuela voy de cinco de la tarde a nueve de la noche,	22	I go to school from 5 p.m. to 9 p.m.,
son cuatro horas solamente.	23	just four hours.
Y después me vengo a mi casa, ceno y hago tarea.	24	And then I come home, have dinner, and do homework.
Esta rutina la tengo de lunes a jueves.	25	This is my routine from Monday to Thursday.
Los viernes son mis días de descanso del trabajo,	26	Fridays are my days off work,
y tampoco tengo clases en la escuela.	27	and I don't have classes at school either.
Los viernes me levanto un poco más tarde:	28	On Fridays I wake up a little later:
me levanto como a las ocho o nueve.	29	I wake up around at eight or nine.
y aprovecho para ayudarle a mi mamá a limpiar la casa.	30*	and I take time to help my mom clean the house.
También los viernes aprovecho a hacer los mandados que...	31	Also, I take advantage of Fridays to run some errands, that...
de como de ir al banco o comprar cosas personales.	32	like going to the bank or buying personal stuff.
También me gusta eh... salir con mis amigos.	33	I also like uh... hanging out with my friends.
Me gusta ir a la playa.	34	I like going to the beach.

Y... el viernes es mi día para relajarme, para consentirme.	35	And... Friday is my day to relax, to pamper myself.
Los sábados y domingos tengo que trabajar.	36	I have to work Saturdays and Sundays.
Los sábados normalmente salgo temprano.	37	On Saturdays I usually get off [work] early.
salgo más o menos como a las doce o una.	38	I get off around twelve or one.
Y después aprovecho para hacer tarea.	39	And then I take some time to do homework.
Me vengo a mi casa y hago tarea.	40	I come home and do homework.
Los domingos sí salgo más tarde del trabajo—	41	On Sundays I get off work later—
salgo como a las dos o tres	42	I get off around two or three.
Pero normalmente hago planes con mis amigos para salir a pasear.	43	But I usually make plans with my friends to go hang out.
Esa es mi rutina de la semana.	44	That's my weekly routine.

*30 It would also be correct to say *ayudarla* (with a direct object pronoun), although this is rare in Mexican Spanish.

Vocabulary

1. usually[1] _____
2. to bathe[4] _____
3. to put on make-up[5] _____
4. to go by[8] _____
5. everyone[18] _____
6. to get ready to[19] _____
7. day off work[26] _____
8. to take time to[30] _____
9. to run errands[31] _____
10. to pamper oneself[35] _____
11. to make plans[43] _____

Translate

1. Fui la primera *en / a* hacerlo.
2. Cecilia se despertó *fresca / frescamente* por la mañana.
3. *Hazte / Haz* la maleta para irte al gimnasio.
4. Recojo a mi amigo *de / en* su casa.
5. Hoy es mi día *a / para* relajarme.
6. Melanie aprovecha *para / por* hacer sus tareas.

True or False: 1. T[2] 2. F[10-11] 3. T[16] 4. F[31, 40] 5. F[25, 36] **Expressions:** a veces - sometimes / antes de - before / así es que - so, therefore / de la noche - at night / de la tarde - in the afternoon / lo más temprano que - the earliest that / más o menos - more or less, around / para - in order to / también - also, as well / tampoco - either, neither / tengo que - I have to / un poco más tarde - a little later **Multiple Choice:** 1. a[10], c[16], d[22] 2. a[38], c[42] 3. d[28-31] **Vocabulary:** 1. normalmente 2. bañarse 3. maquillarse 4. pasar por 5. cada quien 6. arreglarse para 7. día de descanso del trabajo 8. aprovechar 9. hacer mandados 10. consentirse 11. hacer planes **Translate:** 1. en[2] I was the first one to do it. 2. fresca[4] Cecelia woke up fresh in the morning. 3. haz[6] Pack your bag to go to the gym. 4. en[9] I pick up my friend from his house. 5. para[35] Today's my day to relax. 6. para[30,39] Melanie takes (advantage of the) time to do her homework.

notes

La Rutina Diaria de Jared

True or False

1. Jared's grandmother thinks he is lazy.   T ☐ F ☐
2. He is currently working on his thesis (dissertation).   T ☐ F ☐
3. He goes to bed late and gets up early.   T ☐ F ☐
4. He is taking classes on Mondays and Wednesdays.   T ☐ F ☐
5. He is studying advertising.   T ☐ F ☐

Expressions

ahora mismo	actually
bueno	and after that
entonces	and so
lo que sea	anyway
no es que...	but (rather)
o sea	it's not that...
realmente	right now
sino que	so
y así	that is; I mean
y luego de eso	well
y na'	whatever (it might be)

Multiple Choice

1. After Jared gets up, he ___.

   a. has breakfast   c. works on his thesis
   b. has lunch   d. goes for a run

2. Jared likes to ___ on the computer.

   a. practice graphic design   c. post dance videos
   b. blog about his life   d. watch videos to learn languages

3. Jared teaches classes in ___ and ___.

   a. graphic design   c. advertising
   b. theater   d. dance

Text

Mi rutina diaria. Okey, déjenme explicarles mi rutina diaria.	1	My daily routine. Okay, let me tell you about my daily routine.
Yo... realmente, me despierto muy tarde.	2	I... I actually wake up very late.
No es que me despierte tarde porque soy muy vago.	3	It's not that I wake up late because I'm very lazy.
Mi abuela dice que yo soy vago pero...	4	My grandmother says I'm lazy but...

Yo... yo me estoy despertando generalmente a las once de la mañana, doce del mediodía y así...	5	I... I usually wake up at 11 a.m., 12 noon and so...
¿Por qué? Porque ahora yo estoy en tesis,	6	Why? Because now I am doing my thesis.
Entonces, me despiert-... me duermo, perdón, muy tarde haciendo tesis.	7	So, I wake up... I go to sleep, sorry, very late [because I'm] working on my thesis.
Y me despierto muy temprano porque, no... o sea, me despierto muy tarde porque no tengo nada que hacer.	8	And I wake up very early because, no... I mean, I wake up very late because I have nothing to do.
Entonces, okey, me despierto tarde, como, porque ya no hay tiempo para desayunar sino que como la comida de las doce.	9	So, okay, I wake up late, like, because there is no time to have breakfast, but instead I eat lunch at twelve.
Y luego de eso... luego de eso me quedo... me quedo haciendo lo que sea en la computadora.	10	And after that... after that I keep... I keep doing whatever on the computer.
Puede ser: viendo videos, o puede ser trabajando en la misma tesis.	11	It might be: watching videos, or maybe working on the same thesis.
Pero... también usualmente me pongo a hacer tutoriales o a trabajar en Photoshop o en Illustrator... de Adobe,	12	But... I usually also start to do tutorials or work in Photoshop or Illustrator... from Adobe,
porque me interesa el diseño gráfico como soy publicista... estudio publicidad.	13	because I am interested in graphic design since I am an advertiser... I study advertising.
Entonces, es una parte íntegra, es realmente, una parte importante para mí aprender eso y...	14	So, it is an integral part, actually, an important part for me to learn that and...
Bueno, realmente, luego de eso en las tardes doy clases de baile los lunes y miércoles.	15	Well, actually, after that in the evenings I teach dance classes on Mondays and Wednesdays.
Doy clases de baile eh... street jazz. Doy clases de street jazz... de baile.	16	I teach dance eh... street jazz. I teach street jazz... dance.
Y los fines de semana también doy clases de... de... teatro.	17	And on weekends I also teach... theater classes.
Y cuando no estoy dando clases de baile estoy trabajando en mi tesis y...	18	And when I'm not teaching dance I'm working on my thesis and...
Bueno, realmente esa es mi rutina del día.	19	Well, really that's my daily routine.
Eh... Después yo no hago más nada... o sea ahora mismo estoy en tesis.	20	Uh... After that I do nothing... I mean right now I'm working on my thesis.
Termino mi tesis y na', veo cuando entro a trabajar.	21	I'm finishing up my thesis and anyway, I'll see when I start working.

Vocabulary

1. to wake up[3] _____
2. lazy[3] _____
3. to be working on one's thesis[6] _____
4. to go to sleep[7] _____
5. to have breakfast[9] _____
6. graphic design[13] _____
7. advertising agent[13] _____
8. an integral part[14] _____
9. to teach a class[15] _____
10. weekend[17] _____

Translate

1. No es que no me *gusta / guste,* pero...
2. Si no tengo nada *que / a* hacer, veo la televisión.
3. No tengo tiempo *para / a* ver la televisión.
4. Me quedo *a pensar / pensando* en eso.
5. Es importante para mí *saber / que sepa* la verdad.
6. Entró *para / a* trabajar hace un mes.

notes

Recuerdos de la Infancia

Un Viaje a Angkor Wat

Felipe (Colombia)
267 words (122 wpm)
10

True or False

1. Felipe lived in Cambodia when he was thirteen years old.   T ☐   F ☐
2. He marveled at the vastness of the ocean.   T ☐   F ☐
3. He had to explain to the waiter what a hamburger was.   T ☐   F ☐
4. They went back home later the same day.   T ☐   F ☐
5. He was impressed with the temples of Angkor Wat.   T ☐   F ☐

Expressions

ambos	anyway, ...
el día siguiente	both
en fin, ...	didn't have the slightest idea about what
nada que ver con	it looked like
no tenía ni la menor idea de lo que...	it turned out that
parecía como	nothing like
por ningún lado	nowhere
que he visto en toda mi vida	that I have ever seen
resultó que	the next day
río arriba	up river

Multiple Choice

1. Felipe went to Angkor Wat ___.

   a. with his family   c. on a school trip
   b. with some friends   d. *none of the above*

2. They traveled to Angkor Wat by ___.

   a. bus   b. boat   c. plane   d. horse

3. For dinner, Felipe ordered a hamburger but got ___.

   a. a tuna sandwich   c. a plate of bread, meat, and vegetables
   b. pizza   d. a bowl of rice and vegetables

Text

¿Un recuerdo de infancia?	1	A childhood memory?
Bueno, cuando eh... tenía trece años, estaba viviendo en Cambodia, en Phnom Penh.	2	Okay, when I was uh... thirteen years old, I was living in Cambodia, in Phnom Penh.
Y había planeado... había... iba a ir a un viaje a Angkor Wat.	3	And there was a plan to... I was going to go on a trip to Angkor Wat,

y entonces, resultó que la familia no podía ir conmigo.	4	and then, something happened and the family couldn't go with me.
Entonces, me terminaron mandando con la persona que cuidaba la casa.	5	So, they ended up sending me with the person that looked after the house.
Entonces era como… como el guardia de la casa.	6	So, it was like… like the house guard.
En fin, entonces, primero teníamos que llegar allá en un barco.	7	Anyways, so, first we had to get there by boat.
Teníamos que ir río arriba—creo que era el Tonlé Sap.	8	We had to go up river—I think it was the Tonlé Sap.
Y era increíble porque cuando estábamos en el barco,	9	And it was incredible because when we were on the boat,
yo miraba hacia ambos lados,	10	I was looking to both sides,
y ¡no veía tierra firme por ningún lado!	11	and I couldn't see land anywhere!
Parecía como un océano.	12	It looked like an ocean.
¡Era una vaina inmensa!	13	It was something huge!
Y bueno, cuando llegamos a Siem Reap, era la hora de la comida.	14	And then, when we arrived in Siem Reap, it was dinner time.
Y me llevaron… me llevó a un restaurante este muchacho,	15	and they took me… he took me this guy, to a restaurant.
Y… y yo quería comer hamburguesa.	16	And… and I wanted to eat a hamburger.
Y había un problema y era que… el mesero no entendía lo que era una hamburguesa.	17	And there was a problem and it was that… the waiter had no idea what a hamburger was.
Entonces yo le expliqué que era pan con carne y vegetales.	18	So, I explained to him that it was bread with meat and vegetables.
Y el… y el mesero fue y volvió con un plato con pan, carne y vegetales,	19	And… and the waiter went away and returned with a plate with bread, meat, and vegetables,
¡pero nada que ver con una hamburguesa!	20	but it was nothing like a hamburger!
Era todo puesto encima del plato.	21	It was all [just] put there on the plate.
Así… o sea, el tipo no tenía ni la menor idea de lo que era una hamburguesa,	22	Like that, I mean… the guy had no idea what a hamburger was,
y eso me pareció increíble.	23	and I thought that was incredible.
Luego el día siguiente pues visitamos los templos.	24	Then, the next day we visited the temples.
y bueno, ¡estuvo genial!	25	And, well, it was great!
La vaina más espectacular que he visto en toda mi vida fue haber estado por los doce templos de Angkor Wat.	26	The most spectacular thing I have ever seen was having been around the twelve temples of Angkor Wat.
Eh… Bueno, esa es una de las memorias que nun-… nunca se me va a olvidar.	27	Uh… Well, that is one memory I will nev-… never forget.

Vocabulary

1. memory[1] _____
2. childhood[1] _____
3. to plan[3] _____
4. to look after[5] _____
5. guard[6] _____
6. boat[9] _____
7. thing[13] _____

8. huge[13] _____
9. meal time[14] _____
10. hamburger[16] _____
11. waiter[17] _____
12. great[25] _____
13. temple[24] _____
14. spectacular[26] _____

Translate

1. Resultó *que / de que* no no podíamos ir con él.
2. El barco fue *arriba el río / río arriba.*
3. El guardia cuida *por / -* la casa.
4. No tiene nada que *ver / hacer* con eso.
5. Eso me *parezó / pareció* increíble.
6. Visité *los / a los* templos.

---

notes

_____
_____
_____
_____
_____
_____
_____
_____
_____

True or False: 1. T[2] 2. F[8, 12] 3. T[17-18] 4. F[24] 5. T[26] **Expressions:** ambos - both / el día siguiente - the next day / en fin, ... - anyway, ... / nada que ver con - nothing like / no tenía ni la menor idea de lo que... - didn't have the slightest idea about what / parecía como - it looked like / por ningún lado - nowhere / que he visto en toda mi vida - that I have ever seen / resultó que - it turned out that / río arriba - up river **Multiple Choice:** 1. d[5] 2. b[7-8] 3. c[19] **Vocabulary:** 1. recuerdo 2. infancia 3. planear 4. cuidar 5. guardia 6. barco 7. vaina* 8. inmenso 9. la hora de la comida 10. hamburguesa 11. mesero 12. genial 13. templo 14. espectacular **Translate:** 1. que[4] It turned out (that) we couldn't go with him. 2. río arriba[8] The boat went upriver. 3. -[5] The guard looks after the house. 4. ver[20] It doesn't have anything to do with that. 5. pareció[23] That seemed incredible to me. 6. los[24] I visited the temples.

Un Día de Playa

True or False

1. Chelo was at the beach with her parents and a cousin.   T ☐ F ☐
2. They were on vacation in France.   T ☐ F ☐
3. In the distance, they saw an unidentified object floating in the sea.   T ☐ F ☐
4. A plane crashed near the beach.   T ☐ F ☐
5. In the end, they realized the situation was not dangerous.   T ☐ F ☐

Expressions

al sol
arriba de
así que
cada vez más
conforme
de repente
definitivamente
durante todo el día
en realidad
parecía que
poco a poco
por lo que
por si acaso
por tanto
sin embargo
tanto... como...

above
actually
as, in line with
both... and...
for sure
for that reason
gradually
however
in case
in the sun
it seemed that
more and more
so (x2)
suddenly
the whole day

Multiple Choice

1. Chelo recalls a day when she was ___ years old.

    a. 5 or 6   b. 8 or 9   c. 10 or 11   d. 13 or 14

2. People on the beach were scared at first because ___.

    a. there was smoke coming out of the plane
    b. several planes were flying close together
    c. there were people jumping out of the plane
    d. they thought the plane was going to crash

3. It turned out to be ___.

    a. a bad dream   c. a practical joke
    b. an air show   d. an optical illusion

Text

Tengo varios recuerdos de la infancia.	1	I have several memories from my childhood.
Yo creo que sobre todo familiares o con los amigos más cercanos.	2	I think [they're] mostly [about] relatives or my closest friends.
Sin embargo, recuerdo un día que—no sé si tendría ¿diez u once años? No lo recuerdo bien—	3	However, I remember a day when—I don't know if I was ten or eleven; I don't remember well—
pero creo que estábamos en la playa—sí, creo que mis padres y también mi prima pequeña.	4	but I think that we were on the beach—yes, I think [that I was with] my parents and my young cousin.
Y estábamos bañándonos y disfrutándonos de un día de playa en Valencia.	5	And we were swimming and enjoying a day at the beach in Valencia.
Era verano; hacía muchísimo calor.	6	It was summer, and it was very hot.
Y creo que íbamos a comer allí ese día,	7	And I think we were going to have lunch there that day,
por lo que íbamos a pasar muchísimas horas al sol.	8	so, we were going to be spending a lot of time in the sun.
Sin embargo, de repente todo cambió,	9	However, suddenly, everything changed,
porque en el cielo de la playa, arriba del mar,	10	because we saw a black point in the sky at the beach, above the sea,
vimos un punto extraño que se acercaba a la costa.	11	we saw a strange dot approaching the coast.
No sabíamos muy bien lo que era.	12	We didn't really know what it was.
Todo el mundo empezamos a mirar, tanto mi familia, como las personas que también estaban disfrutando del día de playa.	13	Everyone started looking, my family as well as other people enjoying the day at the beach.
Poco a poco ese punto se aproximaba y se iba haciendo más grande.	14	Gradually, the dot was approaching and getting bigger.
No sabíamos qué era: era un punto negro, pero también, conforme avanzaba, tenía color.	15	We didn't know what it was: it was a black dot, but as it got closer, it had color.
Parecía que era un avión. ¡Sí, era un avión, definitivamente!	16	It seemed to be a plane. Yes, it was a plane!
Estábamos muy asustados porque el avión se acercaba cada vez más a la costa,	17	We were scared because the plane getting closer and closer to the coast,
y parecía que no iba a parar.	18	and it didn't look like it was going to stop.
Sin embargo, hacía unas piruetas extrañas,	19	However, it was doing some strange stunts,
que de repente parecía que subía; otras veces que bajaba…	20	suddenly appearing to go up, then fall.
¡Todos teníamos miedo por si acaso había gente dentro de ese avión,	21	We were all scared in case there were people inside the plane,
y… se estrellaba en el agua o en alguna playa!	22	and… if the plane was going to crash in the water or on some beach!
¡De repente, nos dimos cuenta que en realidad eran juegos aéreos!	23	Suddenly, we realized that it was actually an air show!
Y, por tanto, no había ningún peligro.	24	And, for that reason, there was no danger.

	25	Those piruettes were being done by a professional pilot,
Esas piruetas, las estaba haciendo un piloto... un profesional,		
así que todo fue un susto.	26	so it was all just a scare.
Pero pudimos disfrutar de esas piruetas durante todo el día,	27	But we were able to enjoy these somersaults the whole day,
por lo que fue un día de playa inusual.	28	so it was an unusual day at the beach.

Vocabulary

1. relatives[2] _____
2. cousin[4] _____
3. to go swimming[5] _____
4. to enjoy[5] _____
5. to spend (time)[8] _____
6. to approach[11] _____
7. coast[11] _____

8. scared[17] _____
9. plane[17] _____
10. pirouette; stunt[19] _____
11. to crash[22] _____
12. to realize that[23] _____
13. unusual[28] _____

Translate

1. Lo vi diez *o / u* once veces.
2. En verano hace *muchísimo calor / calor muchísimo.*
3. Conforme *avanzaba / avanzó* el día, me sentía menos cómodo.
4. Lo hice *por acaso que / por si acaso* había algún problema.
5. *Había / No había* ningún peligro.
6. Disfruté *con / de* ese día.

notes

True or False: 1. T[4] 2. F 3. F[10] 4. F[22] 5. T[24] **Expressions:** al sol - in the sun / arriba de - above / así que - so / cada vez más - more and more / conforme - as, in line with / de repente - suddenly / definitivamente - for sure / durante todo el día - the whole day / en realidad - actually / parecía que - it seemed that / poco a poco - gradually / por lo que - so / por si acaso - in case / por tanto - for that reason / sin embargo - however / tanto... como... - both... and... **Multiple Choice:** 1. c[3] 2. d[22] 3. b[23-25] **Vocabulary:** 1. familiares 2. primo 3. bañarse 4. disfrutarse de 5. pasar (tiempo) 6. acercarse a 7. costa 8. asustado 9. avión 10. pirueta 11. estrellarse 12. darse cuenta que 13. inusual **Translate:** 1. u[3] I saw him (*or* it) ten or eleven times. 2. muchísimo calor[6] It's really hot in the summer. 3. avanzaba[15] As the day went on, I felt less (and less) comfortable. 4. por si acaso[21] I did it in case there was some problema. 5. no había[24] There was no danger. 6. de[27] I enjoyed that day.

Una Niña Tremenda

True or False

1. Gisela was a quiet and well-behaved little girl. T ☐ F ☐
2. She hurt herself while playing on a hammock. T ☐ F ☐
3. She had to wear a cast for six weeks. T ☐ F ☐
4. While wearing the cast, she had to sleep on her back. T ☐ F ☐
5. She has had a broken bone more than once. T ☐ F ☐

Expressions

bueno	actually, really
como eso	all that time
durante todo ese tiempo	like that
en otra oportunidad	even
en sí	extremely
inclusive	here and there
para acá para allá	itself, per se
por supuesto	of course
realmente	on another ocasion
sumamente	well

Multiple Choice

1. When Gisela was being rambunctious, her parents ___.

    a. usually ignored her   c. scolded her
    b. told her to go play outside   d. made her sit in the hammock

2. In the fall from the hammock, Gisela fractured her ___.

    a. left collarbone   c. right collarbone
    b. left arm   d. right arm

3. Gisela says that her cast ___.

    a. was uncomfortable and painful   c. was very expensive for her parents
    b. was a good excuse to stay home from school   d. was signed by all her friends

Text

Bueno, quiero contarte algo de lo que... de lo que yo hacía cuando pequeña.	1	Well, I want to tell you about what... what I would do when I was a little girl.
Yo era muy tremenda; yo era una niña sumamente tremenda.	2	I was terrible; I was quite a naughty little girl.
Me la pasaba brincando, saltando; no me podía estar quieta ni un momento.	3	I would be skipping, jumping all the time; I could not be quiet for a moment.
Eh... mi papá y mi mamá siempre me... me regañaban por eso,	4	Uh... my dad and mom were always... getting onto me because of that,

porque yo me la pasaba brincando para acá, para allá.	5	because I would be jumping here and there.
Eh... y recuerdo que cuando tenía siete u ocho años,	6	Uh... and I remember that when I was seven or eight years old,
em... me encantaba por supuesto mecerme en una hamaca que había en la casa, en el pasillo de la casa.	7	um... of course I loved to sway in the hammock that we had at home, in the corridor of the house,
Y me tiré sobre la hamaca para mecerme en ella.	8	And I just threw myself on the hammock.
Y me caí de la hamaca y me fracturé la clavícula.	9	And I fell off the hammock and fractured my collarbone.
Em... lo recuerdo bien. Eh... no me acuerdo realmente de la caída en sí,	10	Um... I remember it well. Uh... I don't actually remember the fall itself,
pero de lo que sí me acuerdo muy bien es de que... me enyesaron.	11	but I do remember very well is that... they put me in a cast.
Y ese yeso tuve que cargarlo conmigo por mucho, mucho tiempo.	12	And I had to wear that cast for a long, long time.
Este... creo que fueron como por seis meses.	13	Um... I think it was for six months.
Eh... era como un chaleco, como un yeso que era como un chaleco que me cubría casi todo el pecho y parte del... del brazo,	14	Uh... it was like a vest, like a vest that was a cast that covered almost all my chest and part of my arm,
porque la clavícula que me fracturé fue la clavícula derecha.	15	because the collarbone I fractured was my right collarbone.
Em... era sumamente incómodo.	16	Um... it was terribly uncomfortable.
Y durante todo ese tiempo tuve que dormir boca arriba,	17	And all that time I had to sleep face up,
que me fastidiaba horrores y me dolía muchísimo.	18	and that bothered me and hurt a lot.
Em... pero bueno, esas fueron una de la... de las cosas que tuve que pagar como tremendura,	19	Um... but well, that's the price I had to pay for my mischievousness,
por ser tan tremenda cuando yo estaba pequeña.	20*	for being mischievous when I was little.
Y bueno, como eso también, pues, muchísimas caídas.	21	And well, besides that, there were also many other falls.
Y en otra oportunidad inclusive me fracturé el otro brazo.	22	And on another occasion even I broke my other arm.
Realmente yo era una niña muy, muy tremenda.	23	I was really a handful as a little girl.

*20 Outside of Venezuela (and possibly nearby Caribbean islands), *cuando yo era pequeño/a* is much more common.

Vocabulary

1. terrible[2] _____
2. to skip, jump[3] _____
3. to scold[4] _____
4. to rock[7] _____
5. hammock[7] _____
6. corridor[7] _____
7. to fracture[9] _____
8. collarbone[9] _____
9. to put in a cast[11] _____
10. cast[12] _____
11. vest[14] _____
12. chest[14] _____
13. uncomfortable[16] _____
14. to annoy[18] _____
15. face up; on one's back[17] _____

Translate

1. Los padres de Gisela siempre la regañaban *por / para* ser tan tremenda.
2. Tenía siete *o / u* ocho años.
3. No me acuerdo *a / de* lo que pasó ayer.
4. Me fracturé *el / mi* brazo.
5. Tuve que ayudarle *mientras / durante* todo ese tiempo.
6. Me duele *horrores / de horrores*.

---

notes

Vacaciones

Un Mes en Japón

Melanie (Mexico)
559 words (137 wpm)   🔊 13

True or False

1. Melanie went to Japan three years ago.   T ☐ F ☐
2. She lost some weight while in Japan.   T ☐ F ☐
3. She talks about the public baths (saunas) in Japan.   T ☐ F ☐
4. She was injured at an amusement park.   T ☐ F ☐
5. Overall, she had a great time in Japan.   T ☐ F ☐

Expressions

a pesar de eso	about a month
al momento de...	almost no, hardly any
anteriormente	at the moment that...
casi no	before, previously
como un mes	finally
desafortunadamente	I mean, that is
este	in spite of that
finalmente	once, one time
o sea	quite the opposite
todo lo contrario	uh, um
una vez	unfortunately

Multiple Choice

1. Melanie gained weight in Japan because ___.

   a. her grandma and aunt fed her a lot   c. she ate a lot of fried food and bread
   b. she loved Japanese food   d. she had a lot of free time to snack

2. Melanie's cousin got onto her for not knowing how to ___.

   a. speak the language   c. use chopsticks
   b. stand on escalators   d. parallel park

3. Melanie was impressed by ___ and ___.

   a. Japanese food   c. how organized the Japanese are
   b. Japanese technology   d. how well the Japanese speak English

Text

Las mejores vacaciones que he tenido fueron hace tres años cuando fui a Japón.	1*	The best vacation I've taken was three years ago when I went to Japan.
Fui con dos de mis primas y una amiga.	2	I went with two of my cousins and a (girl)friend.
Fuimos a visitar a mi tía porque... tengo una tía, hermana de mi mamá, que vive allá.	3	We went to visit my aunt because... I have an aunt, my mom's sister, who lives there.
Duramos como un mes allá en Japón.	4	We stayed about a month there in Japan.
Fuimos a Fukuoka pero también visitamos ciudades alrededor.	5	We went to Fukuoka but we also visited surrounding cities.
Este... em... me la pasé muy bien porque no sabía que esperar del viaje.	6	Uh... um... I had a great time because I didn't know what to expect from the trip.
Sabía que era una cultura totalmente diferente a la nuestra,	7	I knew it was a culture completely different from ours,
pero lo único que yo esperaba era perder peso,	8	but the only thing I was expecting was to lose weight,
porque mi abuelita y mi tía fueron de vacaciones a Japón.	9	because my grandma and my aunt went on vacation to Japan,
Y p-... regresaron muy delgadas.	10	And... came back very skinny.
Pero desafortunadamente me pasó todo lo contrario.	11	But unfortunately quite the opposite happened to me.
Eh... los japoneses acostumbrar acom-... -costumbran comer mucha... muchos mariscos mucho pescado, huevo.	12	Uh... the Japanese tend to... tend to eat a lot... a lot of seafood, a lot of fish, egg.
O había... había una comida también muy rara que eran frijoles fermentados que sabían muy mal y apestaban mucho.	13	And there was... there was also a very strange food that was fermented beans and they tasted really bad and were very stinky.
Entonces, como no me gustaba nada de esa comida eh... comía puras frituras, papitas, pan, y subí mucho de peso.	14	So, as I didn't like any of that food uh... I would just eat fried things, chips, bread, and I gained a lot of weight.
De las cosas más interesantes que se me hicieron del viaje allá, o de las más raras, fue que los baños,	15	One of the most interesting things from my trip there, or the weirdest, was the toilets,
no todos, pero sí en muchos baños, encontrabas solamente un hoyo en el piso,	16	not all of them, but in many restrooms, you would find only a hole in the floor,
Y tenías que agarrarte de las paredes de unas agarraderas para poder hacer del baño.	17*	and you had to hold onto the walls using some handles to use the toilet.
Este... y otra cosa que también me llamó mucho la atención es que los japoneses son muy organizados.	18	Uh... and another thing that really caught my attention was that the Japanese are very organized.
Para... una vez fuimos a... a un centro comercial,	19	For... one day we went to... to a shopping mall,
y estábamos subiendo de... estábamos subiendo por las escaleras eléctricas,	20	and we were going up... we were going up the escalators,
y yo iba recargada de lado derecho—	21	and I was leaning on the right side—
o bueno, no recuerdo muy bien si de lado derecho o de lado izquierdo—	22	well, I don't remember very well if it was on the right or left side—

pero mi primo me regañó.	23	but my cousin scolded me.
Y me dijo que me pusiera del otro lado que... porque donde yo estaba recargada sin moverme era donde todos pasaban rápido, o sea que este...	24	And told me to get on the other side that... because where I was standing still was where everyone [could] go by fast, I mean, this...
Los japoneses... se... tienen como que un lado para irse más lento y el otro de las escaleras para irse más rápido.	25	the Japanese... they... have, like, a side to go slower and the other side of the escalators to go faster.
Bueno, eso me llamó mucho la atención,	26	Well, that really caught my attention,
porque nunca había visto eso aquí en México ni en otr-... ni en Estados Unidos,	27	because I had never seen that here in Mexico, nor in oth-... nor in the United States,
que son los únicos países que había visitado anteriormente.	28	which are the only countries I'd visited before.
Otra cosa que también me gustó mucho es toda la tecnología, todos los aparatos que tienen allá.	29	Another thing that I really liked was all the technology, all the gadgets they have there.
Eh... los menús, tú pedías tu comida por una pantalla qu-... en la mesa y te llevaban todo.	30	Uh... the menus, you could order your food through a screen th-... on the table and they brought it all to you.
Este... y... o también me llamó mucho la atención que las casas estaban muy pegaditas muy juntitas.	31	Uh... and... or it also caught my eye that the houses were very close to each other, very tight.
Y muchas veces como para ahorrar espacio, los estacionamientos de las casas este... subían o daban vueltas,	32	And in many cases as if to save space, the parking spaces for houses uh... would raise up or spin,
como, para, varios carros de varias personas, estacionarlos ahí y ahorrar espacio.	33	like, several people's cars, to park them there and save space.
También algo muy feo que me pasó allá fue que fui a un parque de diversiones,	34	And something really bad that happened to me there was that I went to an amusement park,
y me subí a una montaña rusa, este...	35	and went on a roller coaster, uh...
Y ya estando arriba levanté los brazos, o sea, al momento de bajar,	36	And when we were there on the top, I raised my arms, you know, at the moment we dropped down,
pero se me dislocó el hombro.	37	but I dislocated my shoulder.
Entonces, sufrí muchísimo, porque era un día festivo en Japón.	38	So, I suffered a lot, because it was a holiday in Japan.
Casi no había doctores, y los doctores que había no hablaban inglés.	39	There weren't many doctors, the doctors there didn't speak English.
Y no me podían entender, y fue muy, muy difícil y d-... doloroso.	40	And they couldn't understand me, and it was really, really hard and p-... painful.
Duré como dos horas con el hombro dislocado.	41	I had my shoulder dislocated for about two hours.
Pero llegó finalmente un doctor que sí sabía poquito inglés,	42	But a doctor that did know a little bit of English finally arrived,
y me pudo ayudar.	43	and was able to help me.
A pesar de eso, me la pasé muy bien y fue la mejor experiencia que he tenido.	44	In spite of that, I had a great time, and it was the best experience I've ever had.

*1 *vacaciones:* always plural

*2 *hacer del baño* (Mexican): to go to the bathroom

Vocabulary

1.	to stay[4]	_____	14.	escalator[20]	_____
2.	to lose weight[8]	_____	15.	to scold[23]	_____
3.	to tend to[12]	_____	16.	screen[30]	_____
4.	strange[13]	_____	17.	right next to[31]	_____
5.	beans[13]	_____	18.	to economize[32]	_____
6.	to stink[13]	_____	19.	to spin[32]	_____
7.	fried food[14]	_____	20.	to park[33]	_____
8.	chips[14]	_____	21.	amusement park[34]	_____
9.	to gain weight[14]	_____	22.	roller coaster[35]	_____
10.	hole[16]	_____	23.	shoulder[37]	_____
11.	to grab, hold onto[17]	_____	24.	holiday[38]	_____
12.	to go to the bathroom[17]	_____	25.	painful[40]	_____
13.	to catch one's attention[18]	_____			

Translate

1. José se fue a Europa *a / para* estudiar música.
2. Es totalmente diferente *a / que* nuestra cultura.
3. Es todo *lo / el* contrario de lo que se debe hacer.
4. Acostumbro *a / -* levantarme temprano.
5. *Algo me llamó la atención. / Me llamé la atención a algo.*
6. Te quiero *a pesar de / de pesar a* todo.

---

notes

True or False: 1. T[1] 2. F[9-11] 3. F 4. T[34, 37] 5. T[1, 45] **Expressions:** a pesar de eso - in spite of that / al momento de... - at the moment that... / anteriormente - before, previously / casi no - almost no, hardly any / como un mes - about a month / desafortunadamente - unfortunately / este - uh, um / finalmente - finally / o sea - I mean, that is / todo lo contrario - quite the opposite / una vez - once, one time **Multiple Choice:** 1. c[14] 2. b[23-25] 3. b[29], c[18] **Vocabulary:** 1. durar 2. perder peso 3. acostumbrar 4. raro 5. frijoles 6. apestar 7. fritura 8. papitas 9. subir de peso 10. hoyo 11. agarrar 12. hacer del baño* 13. llamar la atención a 14. escalera eléctrica 15. regañar 16. pantalla 17. pegad(it)o 18. ahorrar 19. dar vueltas 20. estacionar 21. parque de diversiones 22. montaña rusa 23. hombro 24. día festivo 25. doloroso **Translate:** 1. a[3] Jose went to Europe to study music. 2. a[7] It's totally different from our culture. 3. lo[11] It's the complete opposite of what needs to be done. 4. -[12] 5. Algo me llamó la atención.[18] Something caught my attention. 6. a pesar de[44] I love you, in spite of everything.

Unas Vacaciones en Praga

Chelo (Spain)
346 words (158 wpm)
🔊 14

True or False

1. Chelo's first trip abroad was to Prague.   T ☐ F ☐
2. She went to Prague to visit her boyfriend.   T ☐ F ☐
3. She regrets not getting an international youth card before going.   T ☐ F ☐
4. They visited other cities besides Prague on their trip.   T ☐ F ☐
5. She can speak German.   T ☐ F ☐

Expressions

a pie	best of all
así que	especially
desde entonces	even
desde pequeño/a	for the first time
hasta hace unos meses	however
incluso	I'd always wanted to
lo mejor de todo	it's worth...
por Internet	on foot
por lo que	on the Internet
por primera vez	since I was a child
pues	since then
siempre había querido	so, therefore (x2)
sin embargo	until a few months ago
sin necesidad de	well
sobre todo	without having to
vale la pena...	

Multiple Choice

1. Which of the following is true?

   a. They got married while in Prague.
   b. She hadn't realized Kafka was from Prague before the trip.
   c. They visited the city of Dresden.
   d. They found a hotel by walking around.

2. Their hotel was ___.

   a. conveniently located in town
   b. far from the city center
   c. Kafka's childhood home
   d. the most expensive part of the trip

3. Chelo said the best part of the trip was ___.

   a. the daytrip to Germany
   b. not having to wait in lines
   c. visiting sites from Kafka's books
   d. her boyfriend declaring his love for her

Text

Escoger solamente unas vacaciones para mí, creo que no es posible,	1	For me to choose just one vacation, I don't think it's possible,
porque desde pequeña he pasado mis vacaciones de verano con mis padres en la playa,	2	because since I was a child I spent my summer vacations with my parents on the beach,
siempre en la zona de Alicante, Denia, o incluso también en Mallorca e Ibiza, en las Islas Baleares.	3	always in the Alicante or Denia areas, or even Mallorca or Ibiza, on the Balearic Islands.
Así que me encanta la playa y siempre recuerdo las vacaciones de verano con muchísimo cariño.	4	So, I love the beach, and I always remember my summer vacations with great affection.
Sin embargo, a los catorce años salí por primera vez de mi país.	5	However, at fourteen I left my country for the first time.
Desde entonces, he estado viajando todo lo que he podido, sobre todo por Europa.	6	Since then, I've been traveling as much as I've been able to, especially in Europe.
Mi último viaje fue a Praga.	7	My last trip was to Prague.
Bueno, siempre había querido viajar a Praga,	8	Well, I had always wanted to travel to Prague,
pero hasta hace unos meses no había estado nunca en la República Checa.	9	but until a few months ago he had never been in the Czech Republic.
Mi novio y yo compramos los billetes de avión cuatro meses antes,	10	My boyfriend and I bought airline tickets four months earlier,
y pasamos todo ese tiempo organizando el viaje:	11	and we spent all that time organizing the trip:
elegimos el hotel, los lugares que queríamos visitar, excursiones que haríamos desde Praga.	12	We chose the hotel, the places we wanted to visit, excursions we'd make from Prague.
Nuestro hotel estaba situado en la Plaza Wenceslao,	13	Our hotel was located in Wenceslas Square,
por lo que pudimos recorrer la ciudad a pie sin problemas y sin necesidad de coger el metro.	14	so we could walk around the city without problems and without having to take the subway.
Antes de ir, bueno, em... antes de ir sacamos las entradas de los lugares que visitaríamos por Internet,	15	Before going, well, um... before going we bought the tickets of the places we'd visit on the Internet,
así nos ahorri-... nos ahorramos las colas para entrar e incluso podríamos ahorrar dinero.	16	so we wou-... we wouldn't need to wait in lines to get in [places] and we were even able to save some money.
¿Un consejo que hay que tener en cuenta?	17	Some advice to bear in mind?
Pues, que si eres estudiante o menor de veinticinco años, puedes conseguir descuentos presentando tu carné joven internacional,	18	Well, if you are a student or under 25 years old, you can get discounts by presenting your international youth card,
así que ¡vale la pena sacar las entradas con antelación y tener ese carné!	19	so it's worth getting tickets in advance and having that card!
Soy una apasionada de la literatura, así que organicé una ruta por Praga,	20	I love literature, so I planned a tour around Prague,

para ver los lugares más emblemáticos de la vida de Kafka, el escritor praguense más famoso de todos, y del que yo había leído varias obras.	21	in order to see the most emblematic places in Kafka's life, the most famous of all Prague writers, whose works I had read several of.
También visitamos otras ciudades del país, como Karlovy Vary y Kutná Hora.	22	We also visited other cities, as Karlovy Vary and Kutná Hora.
¡E incluso hicimos una excursión a Dresde, en Alemania!	23	We even took a day trip to Dresden in Germany!
Me gustó muchísimo ir a Alemania,	24	I really enjoyed going to Germany,
porque así tuve la oportunidad de practicar el alemán, idioma que me encanta.	25	because I thus had the chance to speak German, a language I love.
¿Lo mejor de todo?	26	The best of all?
Fue cuando mi novio se me declaró desde lo alto del Castillo de Praga...	27	It was when my boyfriend declared his love for me from the top of the Prague Castle.
¡Creo que nunca lo olvidaré!	28	I don't think I'll ever forget it!

Vocabulary

1. area[3] _____
2. affection[4] _____
3. Prague[7] _____
4. the Czech Republic[9] _____
5. ticket[10, 15] _____
6. to walk around[14] _____
7. line (of people)[16] _____
8. advice[17] _____
9. to bear in mind[17] _____
10. to get, obtain[18] _____
11. card[18] _____
12. to have the opportunity to[25] _____

Translate

1. *Me recuerdo de / Recuerdo* ese día con mucho cariño.
2. Me gradué de la universidad *cuando / a* los veintidós años.
3. Mi último viaje *fue / era* a Nueva York.
4. Nuestro hotel *estuvo / estaba* situado en el centro.
5. Lo pude hacer sin *la / -* necesidad de preguntar nada.
6. Mi hermano es un apasionado *de / para* los coches.

True or False: 1. F[5-7] 2. F[10] 3. F[18] 4. T[22-23] 5. T[25] **Expressions:** a pie - on foot / así que - so, therefore / desde entonces - since then / desde pequeño/a - since I was a child / hasta hace unos meses - until a few months ago / incluso - even / lo mejor de todo - best of all / por Internet - on the Internet / por lo que - so, therefore / por primera vez - for the first time / pues - well / siempre había querido - I'd always wanted to / sin embargo - however / sin necesidad de - without having to / sobre todo - especially / vale la pena... - it's worth... **Multiple Choice:** 1. c[23] 2. a[13-14] 3. d[26-27] **Vocabulary:** 1. zona 2. cariño 3. Praga 4. la Republica Checa 5. billete; entrada 6. recorrer 7. cola 8. consejo 9. tener en cuenta 10. conseguir 11. carné 12. tener la oportunidad de **Translate:** 1. recuerdo[4] I remember that day with much affection. 2. a[5] I graduated from college at the age of twenty-two. 3. fue[7] My last trip was to New York. 4. estaba[13] Our hotel was located in the (city) center. 5. -[14] I was able to do it without having to ask anything. 6. de[20] My brother is crazy about cars.

notes

Una de Mis Mejores Vacaciones

Jaime (Chile)
364 words (163 wpm)   ⊘15

True or False

1. Jaime went to Huilo Huilo last week.   T ☐ F ☐
2. Huilo Huilo is close to the border with Argentina.   T ☐ F ☐
3. Tourism has had a negative impact on the flora and fauna there.   T ☐ F ☐
4. Villarica is a volcano near Pucón.   T ☐ F ☐
5. Jaime and his girlfriend ate salmon almost every day.   T ☐ F ☐

Expressions

a través de	also, as well
acorde a	although
aproximadamente durante una semana	and also
aunque	appropriate to, in compliance with
de manera apropiada para no	even
el año pasado	for around a week
en pleno verano	however
en vez de	in the middle of summer
igual	instead of
incluso	it is located in
junto a	last year
o algo así	or something like that
se encuentra en	so as not to
sin embargo	through, across
y además	together with

Multiple Choice

1. Huilo Huilo is ___.

   a. a popular beach   c. a biological reserve
   b. an active volcano   d. a small town

2. Jaime likes Huilo Huilo because of ___, ___, and ___.

   a. its environment   c. the architecture of its hotels
   b. the activities it has to offer   d. its fantastic nightlife

3. Jaime and his girlfriend went ___ and ___.

   a. skiing   b. hiking   c. dancing   d. to thermal pools

Text

Una de las mejores vacaciones que he tenido fueron las del año pasado.	1	One of the best vacations I've taken was the one last year.
Estuve aproximadamente durante una semana en un sector del sur de Chile llamado Huilo Huilo.	2	I was in an area in the south of Chile called Huilo Huilo for around a week.

Se encuentra en la Región de los Ríos, que es la décima región de Chile.	3	It is located in Región de los Ríos, the tenth region of Chile.
Fui junto a mi polola y lo pasamos increíble.	4*	I went with my girlfriend, and we had a wonderful time.
Huilo Huilo es una reserva biológica; es un área natural protegida.	5	Huilo Huilo is a biological reserve, a protected natural area.
Está muy cerca de Argentina,	6	It is very close to Argentina,
así que es posible visitar este país a través de este lugar.	7	so it is possible to visit this country through this place.
Lo más atractivo de este lugar es su entorno:	8	The most attractive thing about this place is its environment:
sus bosques, sus cascadas con aguas color turquesa, y además se encuentra en medio de montañas y volcanes.	9*	its forests, waterfalls with turquoise water, and also it is in the midst of mountains and volcanoes.
Como es una zona protegida, el turismo se ha adaptado de manera apropiada para no dañar la flora y fauna del lugar.	10	As it is a protected area, tourism has been adapted properly so as not to harm the area's flora and fauna.
Otro atractivo importante es la arquitectura de sus hoteles;	11	Another important attraction is the architecture of their hotels;
son todos construidos de madera para así estar acorde al entorno.	12	they are all built out of wood in order to be appropriate for the environment.
La arquitectura de estos hoteles es realmente única.	13	The architecture of the hotels is really unique.
En este lugar hay actividades para todos los gustos:	14	In this place there are activities for everyone:
se pueden realizar caminatas, visitar termas, lagos, realizar deportes acuáticos, salir en bicicleta, pasear a caballo;	15	you can go hiking, visit thermal springs, lakes, do water sports, cycling, horseback riding;
incluso se puede esquiar y en pleno verano.	16	you can even ski in the summer.
Otro lugar que visitamos fue Pucón.	17	Another place we visited was Pucón.
Se encuentra aproximadamente a dos horas de Huilo Huilo.	18	It is located around two hours from Huilo Huilo.
Y es uno de los lugares más turísticos de Chile.	19	And it is one of Chile's most touristic places.
En Pucón está el volcán Villarrica, que es uno de los más activos de Sudamérica.	20	In Pucón, you can find the volcano Villarica, one of the most active volcanoes in South America.
Acá las actividades relacionadas con la nieve también son muy comunes,	21	Here, snow-related activities are also very common,
aunque nosotros no somos muy amantes de la nieve.	22	although we don't like snow that much.
Preferimos realizar caminatas.	23	We preferred hiking.
Visitamos un parque nacional que era bellísimo.	24	We visited a national park that was stunning.
Fuimos a piscinas termales en medio del entorno, que era realmente espectacular.	25	We went to thermal pools in the midst of surroundings that were really spectacular.
La vida nocturna en Pucón igual es bastante activa.	26	Nightlife in Pucón is also quite active.

Sin embargo, no teníamos muchas ganas de salir a bares o a la disco.	27	However, we didn't feel like going out to a bar or nightclub.
Preferimos realmente un mayor contacto con la naturaleza,	28	We really prefered more contact with nature,
en vez de salir a tomar algunos tragos o algo así.	29	instead going out and having some drinks or something like that.
La gastronomía igual la disfrutamos bastante—era muy muy rica.	30	We enjoyed the food a lot, too—it was very tasty.
Comimos casi todos los días pescado,	31	We ate fish almost every day,
principalmente salmón que es el pescado típico de la zona.	32	mainly salmon, which is the typical fish of the area.
Y esas fueron nuestras vacaciones.	33	And that was our vacation.
Lo pasamos muy, muy bien.	34	We had a really great time.
Descansamos, conocimos paisajes espectaculares.	35	We rested, got to know spectacular landscapes.
Y eso era lo que buscábamos—estar en contacto con la naturaleza.	36	And that was what we were looking for—to be in contact with nature.

*4 *polola* (Chile): girlfriend

*9 *... además se encuentra...*: Here, *se* is practically inaudible because of the adjacent sounds and Jaime's rapid speech.

Vocabulary

1. area, section[2] _____
2. tenth[3] _____
3. biological reserve[5] _____
4. environment[8] _____
5. to go hiking[15] _____
6. hot springs[15] _____
7. water sports[15] _____
8. to go cycling[15] _____
9. to go horseback riding[15] _____
10. to go skiing[16] _____
11. not to like too much[22] _____
12. stunning[24] _____
13. not to feel like[27] _____
14. (alcoholic) drink[29] _____
15. tasty[30] _____

Translate

1. Disfruté de *mi vacación / mis vacaciones* la semana pasada.
2. Una reserva biológica es un área *protegida natural / natural protegida*.
3. Huilo Huilo está cerca *de / a* Argentina.
4. Se resolvió acorde *con / a* las leyes.
5. ¿Cómo es la vida *nocturnal / nocturna* allí?
6. Me gusta estar en contacto con - / *la* naturaleza.

notes

True or False: 1. F[1-2] 2. T[6] 3. F[10] 4. T[20] 5. T[31-32] **Expressions:** a través de - through, across / acorde a - appropriate to, in compliance with / aproximadamente durante una semana - for around a week / aunque - although / de manera apropiada para no - so as not to / el año pasado - last year / en pleno verano - in the middle of summer / en vez de - instead of / igual - also, as well / incluso - even / junto a - together with / o algo así - or something like that / se encuentra en - it is located in / sin embargo - however / y además - and also **Multiple Choice:** 1. c[5] 2. a[8], b[11], c[14] 3. b[23], d[25] **Vocabulary:** 1. sector 2. décimo 3. reserva biológica 4. entorno 5. realizar una caminata 6. termas 7. deportes acuáticos 8. salir en bicicleta 9. pasear a caballo 10. esquiar 11. no ser muy amante de 12. bellísimo 13. no tener muchas ganas de 14. trago 15. rico **Translate:** 1. mis vacaciones[1] I enjoyed my vacation last week. 2. natural protegida[5] A biological reserve is a protected natural area. 3. de[6] Huilo Huilo is close to Argentina. 4. a[10] It was settled according to the law. 5. nocturna[26] How is the nightlife there? 6. la[36] I like being in touch with nature.

Mi Ciudad

Santo Domingo

Jared (Dominican Rep.)
374 words (110 wpm)   ⊘16

True or False

1. Santo Domingo has a population of about ten million.   T ☐   F ☐
2. There aren't many beaches around Santo Domingo.   T ☐   F ☐
3. Jared says there is actually not much to do in Santo Domingo. T ☐   F ☐
4. Residents of Santo Domingo are suspicious of tourists and outsiders. T ☐   F ☐
5. The city has changed a lot since Jared was little.   T ☐   F ☐

Expressions

como tres millones de	actually
cosas que hacer	all the time, always
debería haber	and that's why
en cualquier momento	at any time
en poco tiempo	I mean; that is
había	in a short time
o algo así	maybe
o sea	or something like that
¿qué mas?	some three million
quizá	supposedly
realmente	there should be
se supone	there was
todo el tiempo	things to do
y por eso	what else?

Multiple Choice

1. Jared ___.
   a. has always in Santo Domingo
   b. grew up in Santo Domingo, then moved away for college
   c. has lived in Santo Domingo since he was seven
   d. grew up in a small town, then moved to Santo Domingo for college

2. What does Jared not say about Santo Domingo?
   a. It's a beautiful city.
   b. It's known for tourism.
   c. It's the second largest city in the country.
   d. It has many foreign franchises.

3. El Malecón is ___.
   a. a shopping mall   b. the boardwalk   c. a traditional dish   d. a local celebrity

Text

Mi ciudad. Okey, ¿qué les puedo decir sobre mi ciudad?	1	My city. Okay, what can I tell you about my city?
Eh... Yo vivo en la República Dominicana.	2	Uh... I live in the Dominican Republic.
Y la ciudad donde... donde vivo y donde crecí se llama Santo Domingo.	3	And the city where... where I live and where I grew up is called Santo Domingo.
Eh... realmente el nombre es un poco más largo, pero vamos a decir que se llama solamente Santo Domingo.	4	Uh... actually the name is a bit longer, but I let's say it's only called Santo Domingo.
Eh... pero es un... es un nombre más largo; usualmente las provincias aquí tienen nombre más largo.	5	Uh... but it's a... it's a longer name; usually the provinces here have longer names.
Eh... ¿qué les puedo decir de Santo Domingo?	6	Uh... what can I tell you about Santo Domingo?
Santo Domingo es una ciudad muy linda.	7	Santo Domingo is a very beautiful city.
Eh... creo que es la ciudad con... con más gente del país.	8	Uh... I think it is the city with... with most people in the country.
Realmente, mi país no tiene tanta gente, eh... quizá diez millones de habitantes.	9	My country doesn't actually have that many people, uh... maybe ten million people.
Pero Santo Domingo tiene que tener como tres millones de esos habitantes.	10	But Santo Domingo has to have like three million of those people.
Em... Santo Domingo es una ciudad costera.	11	Um... Santo Domingo is a coastal city.
Eh... la idea se supone es que debería haber bastantes playas,	12	Uh... the idea supposedly is that there should be enough beaches,
pero lo que hay son... lo que hay son acantilados.	13	but what there are... what there are cliffs.
Eh... eso... es una calle que se llama... le dicen el malecón.	14	Eh, that... is a street called... they call it the boardwalk.
Y ahí la gente se para a ver el mar todo el tiempo.	15	And people are always stopping there to look at the sea.
O sea el malecón bordea la ciudad entera,	16	I mean the boardwalk skirts the entire city,
o sea que en cualquier momento tu puedes bajar hacia el sur y tú vas a llegar al mar.	17	meaning that at any time you can go south and you'll reach the sea.
Eh... bueno, ¿qué más puedo decirles de Santo Domingo?	18	Uh... well, what else I can tell you about Santo Domingo?
Es una ciudad bastante bonita.	19	It's a pretty nice city.
No hay tantas cosas que hacer, realmente.	20	There's not so much to do, actually.
El país se conoce por... se conoce por su turismo y por... y por su calidez.	21	The country is known for... known for its tourism and... and for its warmth.
Realmente, yo creo que eso es bien dominicano de que cuando hay un extranjero, lo intentamos tratar como... como si ellos estuviesen en su casa.	22	Actually, I think that's very Dominican that when there's a foreigner we try to treat them like... as if they were at home.
Y por eso... por eso vienen más. ¡Ja, supongo!	23	And that's why... why more of them come. Hah, I guess!
Y realmente porque nuestras playas y todo eso son muy lindas.	24	And really our beaches and all that are very nice.

Por eso, yo diría que lo más bonito de Santo Domingo es el malecón.	25	That's why I would say the most beautiful thing about Santo Domingo is the boardwalk
Y realmente, el centro de la ciudad ha crecido bastante en... en poco tiempo.	26	And really, the city center has grown considerably in... in a short time.
Yo recuerdo, siendo muy joven, que quizá había en el centro de la ciudad vamos a decir que cinco edificios.	27	I remember, when I was quite young, the city center maybe had let's say five buildings.
Cinco porque yo estaba pequeño, siete años o algo así.	28	Five, because I was small, seven years old or something.
Pero ahora... ahora en el centro de la ciudad se mueve-... se mueven bastantes carros y bastante gente.	29	But now... now the city center bustle-... bustles with cars and people.
Y hay franquicias de... de Estados Unidos y de sitios importantes.	30	And there are franchises from... the US and from important places.
Entonces, realmente ha crecido bastante mi ciudad.	31	So, really my city has grown quite a lot.

Vocabulary

1. to grow; grow up[3] _____
2. coastal[11] _____
3. cliff[13] _____
4. boardwalk[14] _____
5. to skirt, border[16] _____
6. pretty nice[19] _____
7. warmth[21] _____
8. to try to[22] _____
9. to suppose, guess[23] _____
10. franchise[25] _____

Translate

1. Ya *les / los* dije todo sobre mí.
2. China es el país con - */ el* más gente del mundo.
3. España tiene una población de como cuarenta y siete *millón / millones de* habitantes.
4. Se llama Francisco, pero todo el mundo *le / se* dice Paco.
5. La economía se siente como si *estaba / estuviese* en una recesión.
6. La ciudad ha *bastante crecido / crecido bastante.*

notes

San Fernando

Jaime (Chile)
486 words (177 wpm)   ⊙17

True or False

1. San Fernando is a popular tourist destination.   T ☐ F ☐
2. Jaime likes that San Fernando doesn't have tall buildings or big chain stores.   T ☐ F ☐
3. San Fernando is located in wine country.   T ☐ F ☐
4. There are no casinos in Chile.   T ☐ F ☐
5. Nightlife in San Fernando is active throughout the week.   T ☐ F ☐

Expressions

a mi parecer	a couple of
a pesar que	a mixture of
a veces	actually
aunque	also
durante la semana	although
en cuanto a	at time
en realidad	despite the fact that
lo anterior	in my view
lo bueno es que	in terms of
miles de	on weekdays
podemos decir que	related to, concerning
por eso	since, because
por lo tanto	so, therefore
relacionado a	that's why
un par de	the above
una mezcla de	the advantage is
y además	thousands of
ya que	we can say

Multiple Choice

1. It is very common for ___ to visit the thermal baths.

   a. teenagers   c. foreign tourists
   b. elderly people   d. paleontologists

2. Which place is closest to San Fernando?

   a. Santiago   c. Santa Cruz
   b. Termas del Flaco   d. the dinosaur footprints

3. Why do many people leave San Fernando at the age of eighteen?

   a. to go to college in bigger cities   c. to look for jobs in the capital city
   b. to work in wineries in the countryside   d. to take a year off and travel

Text

Bueno, yo crecí y actualmente vivo en la ciudad de San Fernando,	1	Well, I grew up and still live in the city of San Fernando,
que es parte de la sexta región de Chile.	2*	it is part of the sixth region of Chile.
Es una ciudad pequeña de aproximadamente unos setenta mil habitantes.	3	It is a small city with around 70,000 people.
Podríamos decir que es una ciudad tranquila, con pocos centros comerciales,	4	We could say that it is a quiet city, with few shopping centers,
y que es una mezcla de campo y ciudad,	5	which is a mixture of countryside and city,
ya que en sus alrededores hay bastantes zonas rurales.	6	since in its surroundings there are lots of rural areas.
En realidad no es un lugar muy turístico,	7	Actually, it is not a very touristic place,
así que esta ciudad no ofrece muchas actividades entretenidas que hacer,	8	so this city doesn't offer many fun activities to do,
lo que obliga a visitar ciudades más grandes si se busca mayor entretención.	9	so you need to visit larger cities if you're looking for more entertainment.
Lo bueno es que no se han construido grandes edificios,	10	The advantage is that they haven't built large buildings.
y se ha conservado la arquitectura de la ciudad.	11	and the architecture of the city has been preserved.
Esto a mi parecer es positivo,	12	This is positive in my eyes,
ya que no ha habido una invasión de las grandes cadenas que prácticamente arrasan con las ciudades y con nuestro patrimonio.	13	since there hasn't been an invasion of the big chains that practically devastate cities and our heritage.
En cuanto a la actividad económica, podemos decir que San Fernando se encuentra en una zona	14	As for its economic activity, we can say that San Fernando is located in an area
que se destaca por su actividad agrícola y por sus viñas.	15	that stands out for its agricultural activity as well as its vineyards.
Esta zona es muy conocida por sus vinos que tienen muy buena calidad.	16	This area is well known for its high quality wines.
A un par de horas de San Fernando hay un lugar muy turístico que se llama Termas del Flaco.	17	A couple of hours away from San Fernando there's a very touristic place called Termas del Flaco.
Son unos baños termales que se encuentran en la Cordillera de los Andes.	18	They are thermal baths located in the Andes.
Y además es posible realizar diversas actividades: cabalgatas y deportes en la nieve.	19	Also, it is possible to do several activities: horseback-riding and snow sports.
Es muy muy común que personas de la tercera edad visiten estas termas,	20	It is very common for elderly people to visit these thermal baths,
ya que tratan enfermedades respiratorias o relacionadas a los huesos.	21	since they treat respiratory or bone illnesses,
Por eso son tan conocidas en la región.	22	That's why they are very known in the region.
También son muy conocidas, ya que es un lugar de descubrimiento paleontológico.	23	Also, they are well-known for being a place of paleontological findings.

Cerca de las termas hay huellas de dinosaurios	24	There are dinosaur footprints near the thermal baths
que fueron declaradas monumento nacional en el año mil novecientos sesenta y siete.	25	that were declared a national monument in 1967.
A sólo unos minutos de San Fernando hay otro lugar que es mucho más turístico y se llama Santa Cruz.	26	Only a couple of minutes from San Fernando there's a much more touristic place called Santa Cruz.
Se destaca por su arquitectura colonial.	27	It stands out for its colonial architecture,
Y además tiene hoteles lujosos, casinos.	28	It also has luxury hotels and casinos.
Es una zona de viñas,	29	It is a wine-producing region,
y además se realizan varias fiestas relacionadas al vino.	30	and also several festivities related to wine take place.
Así que miles de turistas llegan cada año a visitar esta zona.	31	So, thousands of tourists arrive in this place every year.
Bueno, San Fernando se encuentra en la zona central de Chile.	32	Well, San Fernando is located in the central part of Chile,
Siempre se ha dicho que en la zona central se conservan mejor las costumbres propias del campo chileno.	33	It has always been said that in the central area, customs from the Chilean countryside are better preserved.
La vida nocturna en San Fernando no es muy activa.	34	Nightlife in San Fernando isn't very active.
Durante la semana es difícil que haya actividades en la noche,	35	On weekdays, there are hardly any activities take place at night,
aunque los fines de semana siempre hay discoteques o bares a los que uno puede visitar.	36*	but on weekends there are always discos or bars that you can visit.
En cuanto a la educación superior, acá prácticamente no hay universidades.	37	In terms of education, there are practically no universities here.
Por lo tanto, la mayoría cuando cumple dieciocho años,	38	so when must people turn 18,
se va a otras ciudades más grandes como Santiago, que está a dos horas de San Fernando.	39	they go to bigger cities such as Santiago, which is two hours away from San Fernando.
Bueno, a pesar que no sea una ciudad muy grande y que no haya grandes entretenciones,	40	Well, even though it isn't a very big city and there isn't much entertainment,
y aunque no tenga muchos centros comerciales, sigue siendo una ciudad tranquila,	41	and although there aren't many shopping centers, it still remains a quiet city,
que a veces, eso es más importante que lo anterior.	42	and at times, that's more important than the above.

*2 *región*: an official administrative division of Chile.

*36 *discoteque:* more commonly *discoteca*.

Vocabulary

1. sixth[2] _____
2. countryside[5] _____
3. surroundings[6] _____
4. rural area[6] _____
5. chain[13] _____
6. to destroy[13] _____
7. to stand out[15] _____
8. vineyard[15] _____
9. hot springs[18] _____
10. mountain range[18] _____
11. ride on horseback[19] _____
12. old age[20] _____
13. bone[21] _____
14. footprint[24] _____
15. luxurious[28] _____
16. nightlife[34] _____

Translate

1. A mi *parecido / parecer* son los mismos.
2. La ciudad se destaca *por / de* su arquitectura.
3. Es posible - / *de* subir la montaña en cinco horas.
4. El pueblo - / *se* encuentra cerca de la montaña.
5. Lo hizo a pesar que no *es / sea* legal.
6. Cambodia sigue *siendo / a ser* un país pobre.

---

notes

Valencia

Gisela (Venezuela)
568 words (138 wpm)   ⊘18

True or False

1. Gisela was born in Maracaibo.   T ☐ F ☐
2. When she got married, she moved to Valencia, Spain.   T ☐ F ☐
3. Venezuela has 25 states.   T ☐ F ☐
4. The Battle of Carabobo played an important role in the independence of   T ☐ F ☐
   Venezuela.
5. Trincharas is a thermal spring near Valencia.   T ☐ F ☐

Expressions

a bajo costo	about, concerning
acerca de	almost every day
adicionalmente a eso	and then
bueno	as an adult
casi a diario	as I said before
cerca de	besides that
como dije antes	even
como unos	for a while
de resto	I used to go
en las afueras de	in addition to that
entonces	in the 1800s
gracias a eso	inexpensively
hasta hace poco	maybe
inclusive	near
muy cercano a	of course
o sea que	on the outskirts of
por ahí	or so
por los años mil ochocientos	so, then
por supuesto	some, approximately
por un tiempo	thanks to that
quizás	until recently
y luego	very close to
ya de adulto/a	well
yo solía ir	which means

Multiple Choice

1. When Gisela wa young, her parents moved ____.

   a. from Valencia to Maracaibo   c. from Caracas to Maracaibo
   b. from Maracaibo to Caracas   d. from Caracas to Valencia

2. Which of the following is **not** true about Valencia?

   a. It is an industrial city.   c. It is near the coast.
   b. It has been the capital of Venezuela   d. Its population is around two million.
       for over 20 years.

3. Gisela mentions she used to go to ___ a lot with her family.

    a. Negra Hipólita park   c. the Trincheras thermal springs

    b. Lake Maracaibo   d. the beach

Text

Quiero contarte un poquito acerca de la ciudad eh... donde yo crecí.	1	I want to tell you a bit about the city uh... where I grew up.
Bueno, yo nací en Maracaibo realmente,	2	Well, actually I was born in Maracaibo,
que es una ciudad en Venezuela que queda en el estado Zulia,	3	which is a city in Venezuela located in the state of Zulia,
eh... la ciudad del petróleo, donde está el lago de Maracaibo con el petróleo.	4	uh... the oil city, where Lake Maracaibo, with the oil, is located.
Y hace muchísimo, muchísimo calor ahí.	5	And it's very, very hot there.
Eh... pero como dije antes, yo crecí en Caracas,	6	Uh... but as I said before, I grew up in Caracas,
porque me... mis padres se mudaron a Caracas cuando yo estaba muy chiquita.	7	because I... my parents moved to Caracas when I was very young.
Caracas es la capital de Venezuela.	8	Caracas is the capital of Venezuela.
Eh... y luego ya de adulta cuando me casé, me mudé para Valencia, para la ciudad de Valencia,	9	Uh... and then as an adult, when I got married, I moved to Valencia, to the city of Valencia,
eh... donde viví por más de veinte años.	10	uh... where I lived for more than twenty years.
Entonces te voy a hablar de Valencia, ¿okey?,	11	So, I'm going to tell you about Valencia, okay?,
que es lo que tengo más fresco en mi memoria.	12	which is what is fresher in my memory.
Valencia es una ciudad que queda como a dos horas de Caracas, em... de la capital del país.	13	Valencia is a city located about two hours from Caracas, um... the capital of the country.
Eh... pero curiosamente por los años mil ochocientos, por ahí, Valencia fue capital del país por un tiempo.	14	Uh... but oddly back in the 1800s Valencia was the capital of the country for a time.
Eh... es una ciudad por supuesto más pequeña que la capital, mucho más tranquila.	15	Uh... of course it's a smaller city than the capital, and much quieter.
Este... es la capital del estado Carabobo.	16	Uh... It's the capital of the state of Carabobo.
Carabobo es uno de los veinte estados del... del país, de Venezuela,	17	Carabobo is one of the twenty states of... the country, of Venezuela
y se considera... Valencia se considera la ciudad industrial del país.	18	and it's considered... Valencia is considered the country's industrial city.
Tiene un parque industrial muy, muy grande en las afueras de la ciudad,	19	It has a huge industrial park on the outskirts of the city,
eh... donde hay por supuesto muchísimas empresas.	20	uh... where there are of course many companies.
Y eh... ellas han sido por muchos, muchos años em... una fuente de trabajo importante	21	And uh... they have been for many, many years um... an important source of work
para las personas de la zona, para las personas de la región y del estado.	22	for people in the area, for people of the region and the state.

Eh... Valencia queda en la región central del país, en la región norte... central-norte del país, cerca de la costa.	23	Uh... Valencia is in the central region of the country, in the north... north-central region of the country near the coast.
O sea que en veinte minutos, menos de media hora, estás en la playa.	24	So, in twenty minutes, less than half hour, you are at the beach.
y eso es muy sabroso, muy rico.	25	And that is great, very nice.
Eh... gracias a eso yo solía ir con mi familia con muchísima frecuencia a la playa.	26	Uh... thanks to that I used to go to the beach with my family quite a lot.
Eh... Como por el año dos mil trece, o sea hasta hace dos años,	27	Uh... back in something like 2013, so two years ago,
Valencia tenía por censo como unos dos millones habitantes, quizás un poquito menos.	28	Valencia had, according to the census, some two million people, maybe a bit less.
Eh... tiene un parque muy grande y muy hermoso,	29	Uh... it has a very big and beautiful park,
que el pulmón... es el pulmón central de... de la ciudad.	30	which the lung... is the main lung of the city.
El parque se llama Negra Hipólita y... es un parque hermosísimo.	31	The name of the park is Negra Hipólita and... it's a gorgeous park.
Yo solía ir a caminar con frecuencia, casi a diario a ese parque.	32	I used to go for walks in that park often, almost every day.
Un parque realmente muy, muy bello.	33	[It is] really a very, very beautiful park.
Pues y... muy cercano a Valencia eh... está El Campo de Carabobo.	34	Well and... very close to Valencia uh... there is the Battle of Carabobo.
El Campo de Carabobo es muy importante para el país,	35	The Battle of Carabobo is very important for the country,
porque fue donde se desarrolló La Batalla de Carabobo, por allá por los años mil ochocientos veintiuno, este... que fue la guerra...	36	because it was there where the Battle of Carabobo took place, back in the year 1821, uh... which was the war.
La Batalla de Carabobo se considera que fue la guerra que definió la independencia del país, la independencia de Venezuela. Okey.	37	The Battle of Carabobo is considered the war that settled the independence of the country, the independence of Venezuela. Okay.
Adicionalmente a eso, como a quince o veinte minutos de la ciudad de Valencia queda un lugar muy sabroso que se llama Trincheras,	38	In addition to that, about fifteen or twenty minutes from the city of Valencia you find a nice place called Trincheras,
que es un lugar donde hay aguas termales; hay piscinas de aguas termales.	39	which is a place with thermal springs; there are thermal water pools.
Y uno puede ir y pasar el día allí a muy, muy bajo costo.	40	And one can go and spend the day there at a very, very low cost.
Y este es un l-... es un lugar de verdad bien sabroso, muy rico de estar.	41	It's really a... a very nice place to visit.
Em... de resto, bueno, Valencia es una ciudad limpia, una ciudad muy bonita,	42	Um... besides this, well, Valencia is a clean city, a very pretty city,
que se conserva... eh, o se conservaba muy bien;	43	that remains... uh, or used to be preserved very well;
hasta hace poco se conservaba.	44	until a short time ago it was very well preserved.

| Inclusive era considerada una de las ciudades más limpias del país. | 45 | It was even considered one of the cleanest cities in the country. |
| Eh... eso es lo que te puedo contar sobre la ciudad de Valencia. | 46 | Uh... that's what I can tell you about the city of Valencia. |

Vocabulary

1. to tell[1] _____
2. to be located[3] _____
3. oil, petroleum[4] _____
4. to move (relocate)[7] _____
5. very young[7] _____
6. fresh[12] _____
7. oddly, strangely[14] _____
8. quiet[15] _____
9. to be considered[18] _____

10. company[20] _____
11. source[21] _____
12. nice[25] _____
13. census[28] _____
14. lung[30] _____
15. to take place[36] _____
16. pool[39] _____
17. to be preserved[43] _____

Translate

1. Esta es la ciudad *en / -* donde mi padre creció.
2. Viví allí *por / para* más de diez años.
3. Es una *muy gran ciudad / ciudad muy grande*.
4. *Me / -* solía tomar notas en clase.
5. Es posible hacerlo *a / por* bajo costo.
6. Es muy famoso, *inclusive / inclusivo* en los Estados Unidos.

---

notes

La Cultura

Las Fiestas Patrias

Jaime (Chile)
404 words (173 wpm)   ⊙19

True or False

1. Fiestas Patrias commemorates Chile's independence from Spain. T☐ F☐
2. Fiestas Patrias is celebrated in the autumn. T☐ F☐
3. The festivities begin late in the evening and go all night. T☐ F☐
4. *Cueca* and *terremoto* are traditional dances popular during Fiestas Patrias. T☐ F☐
5. Jaime mentions that people tend to gain weight during Fiestas Patrias. T☐ F☐

Expressions

a medida que	along with
además	as (time passes)
conocido como	during the day
de manera excesiva	every year
diría yo	excessively
durante el día	I would say; if you ask me
en la tarde	in addition
es muy común que	in the evening
junto con	it is said that
particularmente	it's very common for
por lo tanto	known as
se dice que	otherwise
si no es así	particularly
todos los años	since, because
ya que	so
ya saben	you know

Multiple Choice

1. Fiestas Patrias is also known as *Dieciocho* because it ___.

   a. has been celebrated since the 1800s   c. is celebrated on September 18th and 19th
   b. lasts for 18 days in September   d. *none of the above*

2. Entertainment centers set up during Fiestas Patrias are known as ___ or ___.

   a. fondas   c. ramadas
   b. rondas   d. chichas

3. During Fiestas Patrias, by law, everyone must ___.

   a. refrain from drinking alcohol   c. stay at home with their families
   b. display the national flag in front of their homes   d. gather in the entertainment centers to sing *cuecas.*

Text

Una de las celebraciones más importantes de mi país son las Fiestas Patrias;	1	One of my country's most important celebrations is Fiestas Patrias,
también son conocidas como "el Dieciocho".	2	also known as "Dieciocho."
Se celebran todos los años el dieciocho y diecinueve de septiembre.	3	It is celebrated every year on the 18th and 19th of September.
Estas fiestas se celebran desde el mil ochocientos once,	4	These festivities have been celebrated since 1811,
y es para conmemorar la formación de Chile como un estado independiente de la Corona Española.	5	in commemoration of the formation of Chile as an independent state from the Spanish Crown.
Todos los años durante todo el mes de septiembre se resaltan las tradiciones típicas de la identidad nacional, particularmente el folclore chileno.	6	Every year during the entire month of September, typical traditions of national identity are highlighted, particularly Chilean folklore.
Si vienes a Chile durante el mes de septiembre es muy común que escuches cuecas en cada lugar que vayas.	7	I you come to Chile in the month of September it's very common for you to hear "cuecas" everywhere you go.
Para la mayoría de los chilenos es su fecha preferida del año.	8	For most Chileans, it is their favorite time of the year.
Se acaba el invierno; llega la primavera; comienza una fecha de celebraciones.	9	Winter is ending; spring is coming; and a time of celebrations begins.
Por lo tanto, todo el mundo anda más contento.	10	So, everyone is happier.
Lo más típico de esta fecha es que se instalan centros de entretenimiento en cada ciudad,	11	The most typical thing on this date is that centers of entertainment are set up in every city,
en los que se pueden realizar diversas actividades:	12	in which you can do several activities:
bailar, ir a escuchar música nacional, ir a comer platos típicos, juegos para los niños, etc.	13	dancing, listening to national music, eating typical dishes, games for kids, etc.
Estos centros son llamados fondas o ramadas.	14	These centers are called "fondas" or "ramadas."
Durante el día y en la tarde es común que visiten estos centros familias completas, junto con sus niños, abuelos,	15	During the day and in the evening is common for entire families to visit these centers, along with their children, grandparents,
y a poco, a medida que se va haciendo más tarde,	16	and little by little, as it is gets later,
va llegando la juventud y terminan ya a eso de las cinco de la mañana las celebraciones.	17	young people start to arrive, with celebrations ending up around 5 A.M.
En esta fecha se deja un poco de lado los tragos tradicionales,	18	On this date, traditional drinks are left aside,
la mayoría toma los conocidos "terremoto" o la "chicha".	19	as most of the people drink the famous "terremoto" and "chicha."
Se dice que los chilenos durante esta fecha pueden llegar a subir dos a tres kilos,	20	It is said that Chilean people during this time may gain two or three kilograms,

ya que la mayoría de las personas come y toma, diría yo de manera excesiva.	21	since most people eat and drink, I would say, excessively.
Mucha carne, mucho asado, mucho vino y muchas empanadas, que es una preparación típica de Chile, especialmente en estas fechas.	22	A lot of meat, barbecue, wine, and "empanadas", which are typically Chilean, especially on this date.
Además, durante las Fiestas Patrias renacen varios juegos tradicionales:	23	In addition, during Fiestas Patrias several traditional games reappear:
Se realizan rodeos, torneos de rayuela.	24	There are rodeos, [and] hopscotch tournaments.
Y es muy común que los niños en esta fecha primaveral eleven volantines.	25	And it's quite common for children to fly kites on this spring date.
Otro hecho que llama la atención, es que es obligatorio colocar la bandera de Chile en todos los edificios públicos y en todas las casas.	26	Another striking fact is that it is obligatory to place the flag of Chile outside all public buildings and all houses.
Si no es así, puedes arriesgar multas.	27	Otherwise, you can risk fines.
Por lo tanto, en cada casa hay una bandera de Chile puesta ya sea en la ventana o en el patio de la casa.	28	Therefore, at every house there's a Chilean flag displayed either in the window or in the yard.
Así que ya saben, si van a visitar nuestro país durante el mes de septiembre, es mejor que se olviden de sus dietas.	29	So, you already know that if you plan to visit our country in September, you'd better forget your diets.

Vocabulary

1. festivity, party[4] _____
2. to commemorate[5] _____
3. to be highlighted[6] _____
4. folklore[6] _____
5. date[8] _____
6. to end[9] _____
7. dish[13] _____
8. youth[17] _____
9. to gain (weight)[20] _____
10. tournament[24] _____
11. hopscotch[24] _____
12. to fly a kite[25] _____
13. to place, put, plant[26] _____
14. flag[26] _____
15. fine (penalty) _____

Translate

1. Estas fiestas se celebran desde *el / los* mil ochocientos once.
2. Es común que *tienes / tengas* algunos problemas al inicio.
3. Se acaba el invierno y - */ se* llega la primavera.
4. Tomé *mucho vino / vino mucho* en la fiesta.
5. A - */ los* niños les gusta jugar.
6. Es mejor que - */ te* olvides de tu dieta.

notes

True or False: 1. T[5] 2. F[9] 3. F[15] 4. F[7, 19] 5. T[20] **Multiple Choice:** 1. c[3] 2. a, c[14] 3. b[26-28] **Expressions:** a medida que - as (time passes) / además - in addition / conocido como - known as / de manera excesiva - excessively / diría yo - I would say; if you ask me / durante el día - during the day / en la tarde - in the evening / es muy común que - it's very common for / junto con - along with / particularmente - particularly / por lo tanto - so / se dice que - it is said that / si no es así - otherwise / todos los años - every year / ya que - since, because / ya saben - you know **Vocabulary:** 1. fiesta 2. conmemorar 3. resaltarse 4. folclore 5. fecha 6. acabarse 7. plato 8. juventud 9. subir 10. torneo 11. rayuela 12. elevar volantín 13. colocar 14. bandera 15. multa **Translate:** 1. el[4] These festivals have been celebrated since the 1800s. 2. tengas[7, 15] It's common (for you) to have some problems in the beginning. 3. -[9] Winter is coming to an end, and spring is coming. 4. mucho vino[22] I drank a lot of wine at the party. 5. los[25] Children like to play. 6. te[29] It's better if you forget your diet. (*or* You'd best forget your diet.)

La Comida Española

Chelo (Spain)
347 words (154 wpm) ⊘20

True or False

1. According to Chelo, gazpacho is the most famous Spanish dish.   T ☐ F ☐
2. Paella is a dish originally from her hometown, Valencia.   T ☐ F ☐
3. Rice is a key ingredient in paella.   T ☐ F ☐
4. People tend to eat at home during the week, and go out to restaurants on the   T ☐ F ☐
   weekend.
5. Fideuà is similar to paella but is made with pasta.   T ☐ F ☐

Expressions

a fuego lento	anything
acompañado de	both... and...
claro	but nonetheless
concretamente	I don't think that
creo que no	it's an excuse to
cualquier cosa	of course
es una excusa para	over a low heat
pero sinembargo	specifically
tanto... como...	together with
vamos	well

Multiple Choice

1. There are several varieties of paella, but traditional paella contains ___ and ___.

   a. black rice   b. rabbit   c. seafood   d. chicken

2. For Sunday lunch, many Spaniards enjoy getting together with family and friends and ___.

   a. going to a nice restaurant in town   c. cooking paella at home
   b. having a potluck at church   d. having a picnic at a park or the beach

3. A dish with veal and pork stewed over a low flame is known as ___.

   a. cocido madrileño   c. ternera
   b. gazpacho   d. *none of the above*

Text

Si hay algo de lo que a un español pueda pasarse horas y horas hablando: es de comida.	1	If there is something a Spaniard can spend a lot of time talking about: it's food.
Creo que la comida española no es tan famosa como la comida italiana, por ejemplo,	2	I don't think that Spanish food is as famous as Italian food, for example,
pero sin embargo, está igual o muchísimo más buena.	3	but nonetheless, it is just as good or much, much better.
¡A los españoles nos encanta comer!	4	We Spanish love eating!

Em... cada zona de España tiene un plato estrella característico.	5	Um... each part of Spain has a characteristic signature dish.
La paella es la comida española más famosa.	6	Paella is the most famous Spanish dish.
Sin embargo, la paella nació en la zona española del Mediterráneo, concretamente en Valencia, la ciudad en la que vivo.	7	However, paella was born in the Spanish Mediterranean, specifically in Valencia, the city where I live.
El ingrediente más importante de la paella es el arroz,	8	The most important ingredient of paella is rice,
pero se puede acompañar con muchos más ingredientes, claro:	9	but it can be accompanied by a lot of different ingredients, of course:
Hay paella de pollo, de pescado, de arroz negro, de marisco, verduras, vamos, de cualquier cosa.	10	You can find paella with chicken, with fish, black rice, seafood, vegetables, well, with anything.
La paella de pollo y conejo es la paella tradicional y es la que más me gusta.	11	Chicken and rabbit paella is the traditional paella, and it's the one I like best.
Los ingredientes son arroz, pollo, conejo y verduras. ¡Está deliciosa!	12	The ingredients are rice, chicken, rabbit and vegetables. It's delicious!
Bueno, creo que no me he dejado ningún ingrediente.	13	Well, I don't think I left out any ingredients.
En España, y más concretamente en la zona de Valencia, es tradicional tomarla los domingos al mediodía, y siempre acompañados de familia o amigos.	14	In Spain, and specifically in the Valencia region, it is traditional to eat it on Sundays for lunch, and always together with family and friends.
Yo creo que es también una excusa para reunirse y pasar el rato juntos.	15	I think it's also an excuse to get together and hang out together.
Se puede comer tanto en restaurantes como en casa,	16	You can eat it both in restaurants and at home,
aunque yo creo que la mayoría de la gente prefiere cocinarla en casa, especialmente en casa de los abuelos.	17	although I think most people prefer to cook it at home, especially at their grandparents' house.
¡A los españoles nos gusta discutir sobre quién cocina la mejor paella! ¡Ja ja ja!	18	We Spaniards usually like to talk about who cooks the best paella! Ha ha ha!
Sí, yo creo que la gente suele preferirla en casa,	19	Yes, I think that people tend to prefer it at home,
porque durante la semana, la gente, como trabaja, suele salir más a comer a restaurantes.	20	because during the week, people, as they are working, tend to eat at restaurants more.
Así que el fin de semana es una excusa para descansar y para estar en casa con la familia.	21	So, the weekend is an excuse to rest and be at home with family.
Eh... otros platos típicos de comida española son el gazpacho,	22	Uh... other typical Spanish dishes are gazpacho,
que, bueno, es una sopa roja fría hecha de verduras,	23	which, well, is a cold, red soup made with vegetables,
la fideuà, que es una versión de la paella de pescado hecha con pasta en vez de arroz,	24	fideuà, which is like paella cooked with fish and pasta instead of rice,
y, bueno, el archiconocido cocido madrileño, que es típico de la zona del centro de España,	25	and, well, the well-known cocido madrileño ("Madrilenian stew"), which is a dish from the central region of Spain,

y lleva carne de ternera y cerdo cocido a fuego lento.

26

and it has veal and pork stewed over a low heat.

Vocabulary

1. part, area[5] _____
2. dish[5] _____
3. seafood[10] _____
4. rabbit[11] _____
5. to hang out together[15] _____
6. to talk about[18] _____
7. to tend to[19] _____
8. very well-known[25] _____
9. stew[25] _____
10. veal[26] _____
11. from Madrid, Madrilenian[25] _____
12. pork[26] _____

Translate

1. *Esta es la más deliciosa comida / la comida más deliciosa que he probado en mi vida.*
2. Me gusta la paella *de / al* pollo.
3. Yo haría *cualquier / cualquiera* cosa para ganar.
4. Yo creo que *es / sea* muy importante.
5. Prefiero *a / -* cocinar en casa.
6. Fue una excusa *para / a* no decir la verdad.

---

notes

[†††††] **True or False:** 1. F[6] 2. T[7] 3. T[8] 4. F[20] 5. T[24] **Expressions:** a fuego lento - over a low heat / acompañado de - together with / claro - of course / concretamente - specifically / creo que no - I don't think that / cualquier cosa - anything / es una excusa para - it's an excuse to / pero sinembargo - but nonetheless / tanto... como... - both... and... / vamos - well **Multiple Choice:** 1. b, d[11-12] 2. c[25-26] 3. a **Vocabulary:** 1. zona 2. plato 3. marisco 4. conejo 5. pasar el rato juntos 6. discutir sobre 7. soler 8. archiconocido 9. cocido 10. ternera 11. madrileño 12. cerdo **Translate:** 1. la comida más deliciosa[6] This is the most delicious food I have tasted in my life. 2. de[10] I like chicken paella. 3. cualquier[10] I would do anything to win. 4. es[15] I think it's very important. 5. -[17] I prefer to cook at home. 6. para[21] It was an excuse not to tell the truth.

La Música y el Baile

Jared (Dominican Rep.)
305 words (114 wpm) 🔊 21

True or False

1. Jared loves dancing merengue.   T ☐ F ☐
2. He credits Fernandito Villalona for making merengue famous.   T ☐ F ☐
3. Bachata is a more upbeat, happier version of merengue.   T ☐ F ☐
4. Most Dominicans actually do not know how to dance merengue.   T ☐ F ☐
5. Dembow is a popular hip-hop club in the capital.   T ☐ F ☐

Expressions

aparentemente	apparently
dizque	compared to
en comparación con	finally
muy del	indeed
por así decirlo	let's
por último	really
realmente	several times
sí	so to speak
vamos a	supposedly; they say
varias veces	typically, very

Multiple Choice

1. Jared says that ___ invented merengue.

   a. Dominicans   b. Haitians   c. Cubans   d. he isn't sure who

2. Jared ___.

   a. prefers bachata to merengue   c. cannot dance bachata very well
   b. does not like dancing to bachata   d. wants to learn how to dance bachata

3. Which does Jared **not** say about dembow?

   a. that he does not care for it much   c. that the rhythm is catchy
   b. that it is repetitive   d. that it originates from the Dominican Republic

Text

¿Qué tal?	1	How are you?
Eh... vamos a hablarle un poquito... bueno voy a hablarle un poquito sobre la música y el baile aquí en la República Dominicana.	2	Uh... we're going to tell you a little... well, I'm going to tell you a bit about music and dancing here in the Dominican Republic.
Em... vamos a empezar por lo bueno, em... la bachata y el merengue.	3	Um... let's start with the good, um... bachata and merengue.
Eh... el merengue es un baile tradicional.	4	Uh... merengue is a traditional dance.
Eh... no... no estoy seguro... no estoy seguro si lo... lo inventaron los dominicanos,	5*	Uh... I'm not... not sure... I'm not sure if... Dominicans invented it,

pero lo bailamos muy bien, y la música la hacemos muy bien.	6	but we dance it very well, and we do the music very well.
Digo lo hacemos porque me siento orgulloso de ser parte de… de una cultura en la que se baile ese género,	7	I say we do it because I'm proud to be part of… of a culture in which we dance this genre,
porque me gusta bas-… me gusta mucho bailarla.	8	because I like it a… I love to dance to it.
Eh… el merengue es una música muy alegre.	9	Uh… merengue is a very lively music.
Se usa mucho en el carnaval aquí.	10*	It's widely used during carnival here.
Y hay muchos artistas que lo… lo han… lo han vuelto famoso, eh… Fernandito Villalona, eh… Juan Luis Guerra.	11	And there are many artists who have… who have… have made it famous, uh… Fernandito Villalona, uh… Juan Luis Guerra.
Juan Luis Guerra también canta bachata, que es otro género un poco más… más triste.	12	Juan Luis Guerra also sings bachata, which is another genre… a little sadder.
Es más triste en comparación con el merengue, pero… pero también es un género muy bonito.	13	It is sadder compared to merengue, but… but it is also a very nice genre.
A mí no… a mí no me gusta tanto bailarlo pero yo puedo bailarlo.	14	I don't… I do not like to dance to it, but I can dance to it.
Es muy del dominicano saber bailar bachata y merengue.	15	It is very Dominican to know how to dance bachata and merengue.
Y por último, vamos a decir que este género a mí realmente no me interesa tanto.	16	And finally, let's say that this genre really does not interest me that much.
Pero… aparentemente es un género muy importante también aquí.	17	But… it seems to be a very important genre here.
Y lo consume m-… mucha gente: es el género del dembow.	18	And it's consumed by… m-… many people: the genre of dembow.
Eh… básicamente, es repetir un sonido varias veces o repetir una palabra muchas veces,	19	Uh… basically, a sound is repeated several times or you repeat a word many times,
y hacer una canción con un ritmito pegajoso y que a la gente le guste.	20	and make a song with a catchy rhythm that people like.
A la gente no le importa la letra realmente.	21	People do not really care about the lyrics.
La letra muchas veces son plebes, por así decirlo.	22	The lyrics are often plebeian, so to speak.
O dicen algo machista por así…	23	Or they say something sexist, so…
Eh… pero es pegajoso sí.	24	Uh… but it is catchy.
Y… y es muy chulo… ponerlo en el carro y escucharla. ¡Ja ja!	25	And… and it's very cool… to put it on in the car and listen to it. Ha ha!
Pero no es algo que yo disfrute dizque wow… demasiado.	26*	But it's not something I enjoy like wow… so much.

5 Merengue is, in fact, originally from the Dominican Republic.

10 Carnival is a festive season celebrated before Christian Lent.

26 *Dizque* is difficult to translate into English. It can sometimes be translated "so-called" or "like" but is more often left untranslated. It is used before a sarcastic exclamation.

Vocabulary

1. dance[2] _____
2. proud[7] _____
3. to be part of[7] _____
4. genre, kind[7] _____
5. to consume, use[18] _____

6. catchy[20] _____
7. lyrics[21] _____
8. plebeian, common[22] _____
9. sexist, macho[23] _____
10. cool, awesome[25] _____

Translate

1. Siempre habla *sobre / acerca* su trabajo.
2. Me siento orgulloso *que / de* ser parte de este proyecto.
3. Hugo es bastante guapo en comparación *con / a* su hermano.
4. Por *lo / -* último, quiero dar las gracias a todos los que me han apoyado.
5. Lo que haces es *maravilloso sí / sí maravilloso.*
6. No es algo *que / -* disfrute hacer.

---

notes

Días Festivos en México

True or False

1. The Day of the Dead is similar to Halloween in the United States.   T ☐ F ☐
2. Independence Day is celebrated on September 16th.   T ☐ F ☐
3. On Independence Day, people gather around city hall to listen to the mayor.   T ☐ F ☐
4. Carnival is a huge party that lasts for two days.   T ☐ F ☐
5. Melanie talks about what she did last year at Carnival.   T ☐ F ☐

Expressions

antes de	after
cada año	and this is to
despues de	at night
en la noche	before
este	every year
esto porque	for example
lo mismo	it is customary that
los demás	mainly
más que nada	supposedly
por ejemplo	the rest of
se acostumbra a que	the same
supuestamente	this is because
y esto es para	um, uh

Multiple Choice

1. Melanie does not talk about ___ and ___.

   a. Cinco de Mayo   c. Carnival
   b. Easter   d. the Day of the Kings

2. On Independence Day, the president of Mexico ___.

   a. visits members of the armed forces   c. has the Mexican flag painted on his face
   b. gives the "Independence Cry"   d. gives a televised speech from his office

3. What is true about Carnival?

   a. It is celebrated throughout Mexico.   c. A king and queen are crowned.
   b. It starts 40 days before Christmas.   d. Children dress up in traditional costumes.

Text

México es un país con una cultura muy bonita y muy tradicional.	1	Mexico is a country with a very beautiful and traditional culture.
Algunos de los días festivos más importantes en México eh... es el Día de los Muertos.	2	Some of the most important holidays in Mexico... is the Day of the Dead.
El Día de los Muertos, la gente acostumbra a visitar a sus seres queridos que han fallecido, en las tumbas.	3	On the Day of the Dead, people usually visit their loved ones who have passed away, at their tombs.
Les llevan flores, su comida favorita,	4	They take them flowers, their favorite food,
o también en sus casas les hacen un altar con su foto, la música que les gustaba escuchar, su comida favorita, eh... las cosas que a ellos les gustaban.	5	or also at home they make an altar with their picture, the music they liked to listen to, their favorite food, uh... the things they used to like.
Por ejemplo, mucha gente pone botellas de tequila, cigarros, o videojuegos, las cosas que les gustaban a ellos.	6	For example, some people set up tequila bottles or cigarettes or video games, the things they used to like.
Esto porque tienen la creencia de que los espíritus de los muertos eh... vienen a... a... a comerse esos alimentos.	7	This is because they believe that the spirits of the dead uh... come to... to... to eat that food.
Otro día festivo en México muy importante es el Día de la Independencia.	8	Another very important holiday in Mexico is Independence Day.
Se celebra el dieciséis de septiembre.	9	It is celebrated on September 16th.
En las escuelas, eh... los niños van vestidos con trajes típicos de México.	10	At schools, uh... children dress up in traditional costumes.
Y se recuerda este... qué se hizo el Día de la Independencia.	11	And [we] are reminded uh... what happened on Independence Day.
Y en la noche, eh... a las doce de la noche, el presidente sale en la presidencia allá en México, en la ciudad de México,	12	And at night, uh... at midnight, the president shows up at the city hall there in Mexico, in Mexico City,
y da el grito de independencia que es más que nada decir ¡VIVA MEXICOO! ¡VIVA ALLENDEEE! ¡VIVA HIDALGOOO! ¡Ja!	13	and gives the "Independence Cry," which is basically just "Viva Mexico! Viva Allende! Viva Hidalgo!" Ha!
Y esto es para conmemorar a los personajes históricos que contribuyeron a la independencia de México.	14	And this is to commemorate historical figures that contributed to Mexico's independence.
El zócalo en la ciudad de México se llena con miles y miles de personas que esperan escuchar este grito por parte del presidente.	15	The main square in Mexico City fills up with thousands and thousands of people that wait to listen to this cry by the president.
Y en las demás ciudades, las personas se reúnen en el ayu-... en el ayuntamiento,	16	And in the rest of the cities, people gather at the cit-... at the town hall,
para escuchar al presidente de cada municipio hacer lo mismo, dar el grito.	17	to listen to the mayor of each town do the same, cry out.
Y muchas personas que quieren festejar pero no les gusta ir al... al ayuntamiento porque se llena mucho de gente,	18	And many people, who want to celebrate but don't like to go to... to the city hall because it gets too crowded,
pues simplemente se va a restaurantes o en la calle con... con sus vecinos.	19	simply go to restaurants or onto the street with... with their neighbors.

Y hacen fiestas, se pintan banderas y bailan.	20	And they have parties, paint flags on themselves, and dance.
Otro día festivo en México, bueno, o… o festividad aquí en México, es Carnaval.	21	Another holiday in Mexico, I mean, or… or festivity here in Mexico is Carnival.
No se hace en todas las ciudades de México, s-… más que nada donde hay puerto.	22	It doesn't take place in every city of Mexico, s-it's mainly held by the coast.
Y aquí en Mazatlán se festeja el Carnaval.	23	And here in Mazatlan, Carnival is celebrated.
Empieza cuarenta días antes de semana san-… de semana santa.	24	It starts 40 days before Holy Week
Y empieza de jueves a martes.	25	And it goes from Thursday to Tuesday.
Es como una gran fiesta en toda la ciudad.	26	It is like a huge party in the whole city.
Hay desfile de carros alegóricos.	27	There is a floats parade.
Y hay coronación de la Reina, del Rey y de la Reina infantil.	28	and the crowning of the queen, the king and the child queen.
Hay carros alegóricos muy padres.	29	There are really cool floats.
Cada año el tema es diferente.	30	Every year there's a different theme.
Y las personas que van arriba de los carros alegóricos van bailando, aventando dulces o regalos	31	And the people on the floats dance, throw candy and gifts
para la gente que va a ver el desfile.	32	to the people who go to see the parade.
Este… después de Carnaval, el día miércoles se acostumbra a que las personas vayan a las iglesias,	33	Uh… after Carnival, on Wednesday it is customary that people go to church,
y se pongan una cruz de ceniza en las frentes,	34	and get a cross of ashes [painted] on their foreheads.
eh… supuestamente porque se arrepienten de todos los pecados,	35	uh… supposedly because they're repentant of all their sins,
o de las cosas que hicieron durante Carnaval.	36	or the things they did during Carnival.
Y es una manera de demostrarlo.	37	And it's one way to show it.
Otro día festivo en México es el Día de los Reyes.	38	Another holiday in Mexico is the Day of the Kings.
El Día de los Reyes se asemeja mucho a Navidad,	39	The Day of the Kings is very similar to Christmas,
porque los padres dan regalos a sus hijos,	40	because parents give presents to their children,
y les dicen que se los trajeron los reyes magos.	41	and tell them that the wise men brought them to them.
Esta festividad se utiliza más que nada en la ciudad de México o en el estado de México.	42	This festivity is mostly celebrated in Mexico City or in Mexico State.
Y… lo festejan, o lo festejaban, más que Navidad.	43	And… they celebrate it, or used to celebrate it, more than Christmas.

Vocabulary

1. holiday[2] _____
2. to be in the habit of[3] _____
3. loved ones[3] _____
4. to pass away[3] _____
5. tomb[3] _____
6. to believe that[7] _____
7. food[7] _____
8. to be celebrated[9] _____
9. costume[10] _____
11. main square[13] _____
12. municipality[17] _____
13. to celebrate[18] _____
14. city hall[18] _____
15. parade[27] _____
16. (parade) float[27] _____
17. really cool[29] _____
18. to throw[31] _____
19. ash[34] _____
20. to repent for[35] _____
21. to be similar to[39] _____
22. the three wise men, the Magi[41] _____

Translate

1. Acostumbro *a / -* visitar a mis seres queridos cada fin de semana.
2. Esto es *más que nada / más nada que* para festejar el cumpleaños de mi hijo.
3. La plaza se llenó con miles *de / -* ciudadanos.
4. Vamos a *aventar / hacer* una fiesta mañana.
5. Es un día festivo que se */ -* asemeja a Carnaval.
6. En la ciudad de México festejaban el Día de los Reyes más que *nada / -* Navidad.

---

notes

La Comida Venezolana

Gisela (Venezuela)
486 words (146 wpm)   ⊘ 23

True or False

1. *Arepa* is a kind of bread.   T ☐ F ☐
2. *Caraota* is the Venezuelan word for 'carrots'.   T ☐ F ☐
3. *Ropa vieja* is a kind of *carne mechada*.   T ☐ F ☐
4. *Pabellón* is traditionally eaten at Christmas.   T ☐ F ☐
5. Gisela is not particularly fond of *hallaca*.   T ☐ F ☐

Expressions

acerca de	about, regarding
como por una hora	as you know
como tú sabes	called
lo que sea	for about an hour
lo que uno quiera	in order to
para	later, subsequently
por dentro	on the inside
posteriormente	whatever
que es	whatever you want
que se llama	which is

Multiple Choice

1. Which of the following is **not** true about *arepa*?

    a. It is made with maize flour.   c. It can be filled with meat, cheese, etc.
    b. It is cooked on a hot pan.   d. It contains fried banana.

2. ___ consists of white rice, *tajadas*, *caroatas*, and shredded meat.

    a. pernil   c. hallaca
    b. pabellón   d. arepa

3. Hallaca is ___ and ___.

    a. wrapped in plantain leaves   c. toasted on a hot pan
    b. cooked in hot water   d. filled with cheese

Text

Te voy a hablar un poquito acerca de la cultura del país.	1	I'm going to tell you a little about the culture of the country.
Y me voy a centrar en la comida.	2	And I will focus on food.
¿Cuál es la comida típica de nuestro país?	3	What is the typical food of our country?
Bueno, la más típica y conocida es la "arepa", como tú sabes.	4	Well, the most typical and famous is the "arepa", as you know.
Una... es nuestro pan—nuestro pan de cada día es la arepa.	5	A... it's our bread—our everyday bread is arepa.
La arepa se hace con harina de maíz.	6	Arepa is made with maize flour (cornmeal).

Eh... se vende en casi todos los países del mundo.	7	Uh... it is sold in almost every country in the world.
Eh... se llama Harina P.A.N.	8	Uh... it's called Harina PAN.
Y con esa harina de maíz, mezclada con agua y un poquito de sal, se hace la arepa,	9	And with that maize flour, mixed with water and a bit of salt, arepa is made.
que son unas figuras como redondas que se pasan por una plancha muy caliente, por un sartén muy caliente que en Venezuela se llama "budare",	10	They are round shapes and are placed on a very hot plate, a very hot pan that in Venezuela is called "budare",
para hacerle una capa tostada de cada lado a esa arepa.	11	to give it a toasted layer on either side of the arepa.
Y luego se deja cocinar por dentro un poco.	12	And then it's left to cook inside a bit.
Y esa arepa, pues, es muy sabrosa.	13	This arepa is, well, very tasty.
Se... se come con mantequilla.	14	You [can] eat it with butter.
Eh... se puede rellenar de lo que sea, de queso, de carne, de pollo, de... lo que uno quiera; de huevo revuelto, lo que uno quiera.	15	Uh... you can fill it with whatever, cheese, meat, chicken, with... whatever you want; scrambled eggs, whatever you want.
Ese digamos que es la comida más típica de allá.	16*	We can say it's the most traditional food there.
Nuestro plato típico se llama "pabellón".	17	Our signature dish is called "pabellón".
El pabellón es el plato de la comida típica de Venezuela que se compone de:	18	Pabellón is the main dish of Venezuela and it includes:
arroz blanco, caraotas—que son las eh... los guisantes negros eh... preparados con ciertos aliños—	19	white rice, 'caraotas', which are... uh... black peas uh... cooked with certain seasonings—
eh... tajada, que es plátano maduro frito,	20	uh... 'tajadas', which are ripe, fried plantains,
y carne mechada, que es una carne que se prepara y se esmecha... eh... se esmecha en tiras.	21	and shredded meat, which is a meat that is prepared and shredded into strips.
Es lo que en otros países, especialmente quizás en Cuba, también en República Dominicana y en otros pa-... países, llaman a esta carne "ropa vieja".	22	It is what in other countries, especially perhaps in Cuba, also in the Dominican Republic and other cou- countries, they call this meat "ropa vieja" ("old clothes").
En Venezuela lo llamamos "carne mechada".	23	In Venezuela we call it "carne mechada".
Entonces el Pabellón es el plato típico de Venezuela que se compone de arroz blanco, tajadas (que es el plátano maduro frito), caraotas (que son los guisantes negros), eh... y la carne mechada.	24	So, pabellón is Venezuela's typical dish, and it consists of white rice, tajadas (ripe, fried plantains) caraotas (which are the black beans), uh... and shredded meat.
Luego para diciembre—que es el tercer plato que te quiero presentar—eh... nosotros tenemos un plato típico que se llama "hallaca".	25	Then in December—and this is the third plate I want to introduce—uh... we have a typical dish called "hallaca".
Esta "hallaca" se hace también con harina de maíz.	26	This hallaca is also made with maize flour.
Eh... Se rellena de un guiso muy sabroso que se puede hacer con pollo,	27	Uh... it is filled with a very tasty stew that can be made with chicken,

que se puede hacer con carne de gallina o con carne de res.	28	that can be made with chicken meat or with beef.
Se hace un guiso muy sabroso,	29	A very tasty stew is prepared,
y se rellena esta masa amarilla.	30	and this yellow dough is filled with it...
Y se envuelve posteriormente en hojas de plátano.	31	And it's then wrapped in plantain leaves.
Esto se cocina en agua caliente como por una hora, hora y media.	32	This is cooked in hot water for about one to one and half hours.
Y se sirve como plato de Navidad y de año nuevo, o en la época de Navidad.	33	And it's served as a Christmas and New Year's meal, or during the Christmas season.
Se sirve la hallaca con pan de jamón, que es un pan muy rico hecho con jamón, pasitas, aceitunas.	34	Hallaca is served with ham bread, which is a really tasty bread made with ham, raisins, olives.
Se sirve con pernil, que es carne de cerdo al horno,	35	It's served with 'pernil', which is baked pork,
y con la ensalada rusa, que es una ensalada que se prepara con papas, zanahoria cocinada.	36	and with Russian salad, which is a salad prepared with boiled potatoes and carrots.
Eh... a veces se le echa pollo esmechado, se le echa guisantes y se le echa un poquito de mayonesa.	37	Uh... sometimes shredded chicken meat is added, and green peas and a bit of mayonnaise.
Ese es nuestro plato navideño.	38	That's our Christmas dish.

*16 Gisela say *allá* because she is not currently in Venezuela.

Vocabulary

1. to focus on   _____
2. flour   _____
3. corn, maize   _____
4. round   _____
5. sheet, plate   _____
6. pan, skillet   _____
7. to fill   _____
8. scrambled eggs   _____
9. to consist of   _____
10. pea   _____
11. seasoning   _____
12. to be shredded into strips   _____
13. stew   _____
14. beef   _____
15. dough   _____
16. to be wrapped   _____
17. raisin   _____
18. olive   _____
19. baked pork   _____
20. carrot   _____
21. Christmas- (adj) _____

Translate

1. La carne se come en todos los países *en el / del* mundo.
2. Posteriormente se deja *a / -* cocinar por dentro.
3. Como tú sabes, solamente estuve ahí *por como / como por* cinco minutos.
4. La comida venezolana se compone de platos *como / cómo* pabellón y hallaca.
5. Me gustan la tajadas, *que / qué* son plátanos maduros fritos.
6. Se sirve con carne *de / -* cerdo.

True or False: 1. T[5] 2. F[19] 3. F[22-23] 4. F[25, 33] 5. F[25-] **Multiple Choice:** 1. d[15] 2. b[24] 3. a[31], b[32] **Expressions:** acerca de - about, regarding / como por una hora - for about an hour / como tú sabes - as you know / lo que sea - whatever / lo que uno quiera - whatever you want / para - in order to / por dentro - on the inside / posteriormente - later, subsequently / que es - which is / que se llama - called **Vocabulary:** 1. centrar en 2. harina 3. maíz 4. redondo 5. plancha 6. sartén 7. rellenar 8. huevo revuelto 9. componerse de 10. guisante 11. aliño 12. esmecharse en tiras 13. guiso 14. carne de res 15. masa 16. envolverse 17. pas(it)a 18. aceituna 19. cerdo al horno 20. zanahoria 21. navideño **Translate:** 1. del[7] Meat is eaten in every country in the world. 2.-[12] Then it's left to cook inside. 3. como por[32] As you know, I was only there for some five minutes. 4. como[33] Venezuelan cuisine consists of dishes such as pabellon and hallaca. 5. que[34] I like tajadas, which are ripe, fried plantains. 6. de[35] It is served with pork.

Día Sin Automóvil

Felipe (Colombia)
291 words (134 wpm) ⊙ 24

True or False

1. At first, people in Bogata did not appreciate Car-Free Day. T ☐ F ☐
2. People are encouraged to stay home on Car-Free Day. T ☐ F ☐
3. Car-Free Day is now mandatory throughout Colombia. T ☐ F ☐
4. People in Bogata seem to enjoy Car-Free Day. T ☐ F ☐
5. Felipe mentions that Car-Free Day is internationally celebrated. T ☐ F ☐

Expressions

en pro de	and besides this
entonces	either... or...
específicamente para	in favor of
está permitido que	is allowed to
la idea es que	it sounds crazy, but
o sea	so, therefore
por lo general	specifically for
pues	that is; I mean
suena como una locura, pero	the idea is that
y además de esto	usually
ya sea... o...	well, then

Multiple Choice

1. Which of the following is not allowed on the streets of Bogata on Car-Free Day?

   a. carpooling   b. parked cars   c. taxis   d. buses

2. People in Bogata like Car-Free Day because ___ and ___.

   a. normally bicycles are not allowed on the main streets
   b. it offers a nice respite from the hustle and bustle
   c. they can participate in various sporting activities
   d. they don't have to go to work that day

3. Bogata's main streets are closed to automobiles ___.

   a. every Sunday
   b. the first Sunday of every week
   c. two or three times a year
   d. on Saturdays and Sundays

Text

¿Algo cultural?	1	Something cultural?
Bueno, en Bogotá en los últimos años se ha fomentado una cultura en pro del medio ambiente,	2	Okay. In Bogota in recent years there has been a fostering of a culture in favor of the environment,
y el cuidado y la limpieza del aire y esto.	3	and the care and the clean air and so on.
Hace algunos años una de las administraciones propuso una idea radical,	4	A few years ago one of the administrations proposed a radical idea,
y se trataba de... que por un día, en toda la ciudad no fuera permitido el uso del automóvil particular.	5	and it was that... for one day, throughout the city, the use of private cars was not allowed.
O sea, solamente podían operar buses y taxis.	6	That is, only buses and taxis could operate.
Y las personas que tenían carro tenían que dejarlo guardado en sus casas.	7	And people who had cars had to leave them at home.
Suena como una locura, pero lo probamos,	8	It sounds crazy, but we tried it,
y nos gustó tanto que ahora lo hacemos como dos, tres veces al año en Bogotá.	9	and loved it so much that we now do it some two or three times a year in Bogota.
La idea es que las personas utilicen menos el... el automóvil,	10	The idea is that people use automobiles less,
y se movilicen ya sea en bicicleta o caminando o utilizando el transporte público.	11	and get around either by bike or walking or using public transportation.
Y esto le da un respiro en Bogotá,	12	And this offers you respite in Bogota,
que por lo general es una ciudad... como es muy grande y con una gran población.	13	which usually is a city... since it is very big and has a large population.
Entonces, tiene muchísimo tráfico,	14	So, it has a lot of traffic,
pero durante esos días es una ciudad muy calmada,	15	but during these days it is a very calm city,
donde se ve la gente haciendo deporte, y...	16	where people do sporting activities, and...
y el aire se siente diferente.	17	and the air feels different.
Otra de las propuestas que se hicieron hace algunos años en otra administración fue la de crear las ciclovías o ciclorutas,	18	Another proposal that was made some years ago in another administration was to create bike lanes or bike paths,
en las que parecido a ciudades como en Europa que tienen vías asignadas específicamente para las bicicletas,	19	where, like in cities in Europe that have assigned routes specifically for bikes,
en Bogotá encontramos una red de ciclorrutas por toda la ciudad,	20	in Bogota we find a network of bike paths throughout the city,
donde solamente está permitido que las bicicletas transiten por allí.	21	and only bicycles are allowed to go along there.
Y además de esto, todos los domingos Bogotá se convierte en una ciclovía.	22	And besides this, every Sunday Bogota becomes a bike path,
pues se cierran todas las calles principales de Bogotá.	23	as all Bogota's main streets are closed.
Se cierra el acceso a los automóviles,	24	Access is closed to cars

y las personas utilizan las vías para montar en bicicleta, en patines, trotar, sacar los perros.	25	and people use the roads for cycling, rollerblading, jogging, walk the dogs.	
Es un día... es para la familia.	26	It's a day... it's for the family.	

Vocabulary

1. to be encouraged[2] _____
2. environment[2] _____
3. cleanliness[3] _____
4. privately owned car[5] _____
5. to leave (something) at[7] _____
6. to offer respite[12] _____
7. calm[15] _____
8. bike lane/path[18] _____
9. a network of[20] _____
10. to ride a bike, cycle[25] _____
11. to jog[25] _____
12. to walk one's dog[25] _____

Translate

1. El gobierno *ha / -* propuso una idea que suena como una locura.
2. La idea es que no *está / esté* permitido que se use el cigarro electrónico dentro de restaurantes.
3. Se puede visitar el pueblo, ya sea en coche *o / ya* en tren.
4. Por lo general, me siento *diferente / diferentemente* luego de meditar.
5. Me gusta ir al gimnasio, y además de esto voy a trotar *todos / cadas* los domingos.
6. Es una película *para / por* toda la familia.

---

notes

True or False: 1. F[8-9] 2. F[10-11] 3. F 4. T[25-26] 5. F **Expressions:** en pro de - in favor of / entonces - so, therefore / específicamente para - specifically for / está permitido que - is allowed to / la idea es que - the idea is that / o sea - that is; I mean / por lo general - usually / pues - well, then / suena como una locura, pero - it sounds crazy, but / y además de esto - and besides this / ya sea... o... - either... or... **Multiple Choice:** 1. a[5] 2. b[12], c[16] 3. a[22-23] **Vocabulary:** 1. fomentarse 2. medio ambiente 3. limpieza 4. automóvil particular 5. dejar guardado en 6. dar un respiro 7. calmado 8. ciclovía, cicloruta 9. una red de 10. montar en bicicleta 11. trotar 12. sacar el perro **Translate:** 1. -[4] The government proposed an idea that sounds crazy. 2. esté[10] The idea is that using e-cigarettes inside restaurants not be allowed. 3. o[11] You can visit the town either by car or train. 4. diferente[17] I usually feel different after meditating. 5. todos[22] I like to go to the gym, and in addition to this I go jogging every Sunday. 6. para[26] It's a movie for the whole family.

Temas Sociales

Los Indocumentados

Jared (Dominican Rep.)
385 words (96 wpm) ⊘ 25

True or False

1. Jared talks about the situation for Dominicans in the United States. T ☐ F ☐
2. The Dominican Republic and Haiti used to have friendly relations. T ☐ F ☐
3. The situation stems from the implementation of a new immigration law. T ☐ F ☐
4. Jared thinks what is happening now is like what happened in Nazi Germany. T ☐ F ☐
5. He believes every country has the right to deport illegal aliens. T ☐ F ☐

Expressions

a la fuerza	and so on; and others
ahora mismo	any other
bueno	by force
cualquier otro	even
digo yo	I say; if you ask me
el punto es que	if I remember correctly
en realidad	in fact
eso sí puedo decir	recently
hoy en día	right now
hubo	so to speak
incluso	that's for sure
lo mismo	the point is that
por así decirlo	the same (thing)
recientemente	there was
si mal no recuerdo	these days
y demás	well

Multiple Choice

1. Which of the following does Jared **not** mention about the history of the Dominican Republic and Haiti?

   a. Haiti gained its independence first.
   b. Haiti has tried to invade the Dominican Republic several times.
   c. Haiti and the Dominican Republic used to be one country.
   d. Haitians have been living in the Dominican Republic for many years.

2. Recently, many Haitians have ___ and ___.

   a. begun a negative campaign against the Dominican Republic.
   b. left the Dominican Republic for the United States
   c. had children in the Dominican Republic so they do can stay
   d. compared the Dominican Republic to the Nazi regime.

3. What is Jared's opinion on the government's decision to deport undocumented Haitians?

    a. It violates human rights.
    b. It is a matter of national sovereignty

    c. The law is very disorganized.
    d. He does not state his personal opinion.

Text

¡Eh! ¿Qué tal?	1	Hey! How are you?
Bueno, ahora les... les voy a hablar un poquito de lo que yo creo son derechos humanos.	2	Well, now I'm going to tell you... you a bit about what I believe are human rights.
Eh... Es un tema bastante importante hoy en día aquí en mi país en la República Dominicana:	3	Eh... It's a very important issue these days here in my country in the Dominican Republic:
los derechos humanos de los haitianos.	4	the human rights of Haitians.
¿Qué pasa?	5	What's happening?
Ese es un tema... es que es un tema bastante largo.	6	That's an issue... it's a pretty long story.
Eh... Los haitianos tienen mucho tiempo aquí,	7	Uh... Haitians have been here a long time.
incluso eh... ellos fueron los primeros en conseguir la independencia, ¿si? como nación.	8	They were even uh... the first to gain independence, right, as a nation.
Y nosotros les seguimos el paso a ellos.	9	And we followed their path.
Ellos incluso nos ayudaron a... a volvernos nación independiente.	10	They even helped us to become an independent country.
Pero que pasa eh... hace ya bastantes, varios, muchos años—ahora mismo no recuerdo,	11	But what has been happening, eh... several, many years ago—I can't remember right now,
hemos tenido una mala... una mala... nos llevamos mal.	12	we had a bad... bad... we don't get along.
Nos llevamos mal con los haitianos como país,	13	We don't get along with Haitians as country,
no... no puedo decir yo como persona pero realmente,	14	I... I cannot say as a person but really,
hubo... hubo una... hubo una..., si mal no recuerdo, una o varias invasión-... invasiones haitianas.	15	there... there was a... there was a..., if I remember correctly, one or several invasions... Haitian invasions.
Entonces, eso... eso como que... realmente, hizo que la relación entre mi país y Haiti em... cortaran... cortaran la relación.	16	So, that... that like that... really made the relations between my country and Haiti um... break off... [made] them break off relations.
Entonces, bueno, el punto es que muchos haitianos han vivido muchos años aquí,	17	Then, well, the point is that many Haitians have lived here for many years,
y recientemente eh... mi país ha puesto una ley migratoria que dice que los... los haitianos que estén... que estén indocumentados se irían a su país.	18	and recently uh... my country has imposed an immigration law that says that Haitians that are... that are undocumented immigrants would go back to their country.
Pero ¿qué pasa?	19	But what happens?
Los haitianos fuera de aquí... fuera de... del Caribe, en EEUU y demás, han logrado crear una campaña de boicot, por así decirlo,	20	Haitians in other places... outside the... the Caribbean, in the U.S. and other places, have

		managed to create a boycott campaign, so to speak,
una campaña de desinformación y de difamación de la República Dominicana,	21	a campaign of disinformation and defamation against the Dominican Republic,
diciendo que nosotros... diciendo que nosotros... nosotros los estamos llevando a la fuerza de aquí para su país,	22	saying we... saying we... are carrying them by force from here to their country,
que los estamos tratando mal,	23	that we are treating them badly,
que... comparándonos con el régimen nazi,	24	that... comparing us to the Nazi regime,
cuando en realidad ellos han tenido bastante tiempo para recoger sus documentos y demostrar que si son ciudadanos dominicanos,	25	when in fact they have had enough time to gather their documents and prove if they are Dominican citizens,
o que tienen hijos aquí y que se pueden quedar.	26	or have children here and can stay.
Pero realmente, cualquier otro país hace lo mismo.	27	But really, any other country does the same.
Estados Unidos puede, por ejemplo, hacer lo mismo con los mexicanos o con... realmente con cualquiera.	28	The United States can, for example, do the same with Mexicans or with... really with anyone.
Cualquier otro país tiene derecho a deportar, enviar... a los ilegales.	29	Any country has the right to deport, send away... illegals.
Entonces, mi país es un país muy desorganizado, muy desorganizado.	30	You know, my country is a very disorganized country, very disorganized.
Eso sí puedo decir,	31	That I can say [for sure],
pero ahora que se quiere organizar han creado como esta campaña negativa hacia nosotros,	32	but now that we want to organize, they have created this negative campaign toward us,
cuando, realmente, nadie puede tocar la... lo que es la soberanía nacional, digo yo.	33	when, really, nobody can touch... what is national sovereignty, I say.
Es mi opinión en el tema.	34	It's my opinion on the subject.

Vocabulary

1. human rights[2] _____
2. issue[3] _____
3. Haitian[4] _____
4. to have been here a long time[7] _____
5. to follow one's lead[9] _____
6. boycotting campaign[20] _____
7. defamation[21] _____
8. to gather[25] _____
9. to prove[25] _____
10. to have the right to[29] _____
11. disorganized[30] _____
12. sovereignty[33] _____

Translate

1. Jared nos habló de lo que él cree *que / -* es un tema muy importante.
2. Hay muchos *Haitianos / haitianos* indocumentados en el país.
3. La campaña hizo que las relaciones se *cortaran / cortaron* entre los dos países.
4. Jared compara la situación *a / con* la de otros países.
5. Ya has tenido *tiempo bastante / bastante tiempo* para terminar el proyecto.
6. Jared da su opinión *de / en* el tema.

notes

True or False: 1. F[4] 2. T[10] 3. T[18] 4. F[21-24] 5. T[29] **Expressions:** a la fuerza - by force / ahora mismo - right now / bueno - well / cualquier otro - any other / digo yo - I say; if you ask me / el punto es que - the point is that / en realidad - in fact / eso sí puedo decir - that's for sure / hoy en día - these days / hubo - there was / incluso - even / lo mismo - the same (thing) / por así decirlo - so to speak / recientemente - recently / si mal no recuerdo - if I remember correctly / y demás - and so on; and others **Multiple Choice:** 1. c[8, 15, 17] 2. a[20-21], d[24] 3. b[33] **Vocabulary:** 1. derechos humanos 2. tema 3. haitiano 4. tener mucho tiempo aquí 5. seguir el paso a 6. campaña de boicot 7. difamación 8. recoger 9. demostrar 10. tener derecho a 11. desorganizado 12. soberanía **Translate:** 1. -[2] Jared told us about what he believes is an important issue. 2. haitianos[4] There are a lot of undocumented Haitians in the country. 3. cortaran[16] The campaign caused a breakdown in the relationship between the two countries. 4. con[24] Jared compares the situation to that of other countries. 5. bastante tiempo[25] 6. en[34] Jared gives his opinion on the subject.

La Violencia en México

True or False

1. Violence is on the rise in Mexico.   T ☐ F ☐
2. Crime related to drug trafficking is actually just a small portion of the overall   T ☐ F ☐
   crime in Mexico.
3. The level of violence and guns present in Mexican schools worries Melanie.   T ☐ F ☐
4. Melanie implies that if you are not involved in drug trafficking, you will not   T ☐ F ☐
   see much violence in Mexico.
5. Melanie credits teh government and media for helping to improve non-drug   T ☐ F ☐
   trafficking related violence.

Expressions

de ahí en fuera	actually
de hecho	in reality
en cuanto a	in recent years
en ese aspecto	in terms of
en los últimos años	in that respect
en realidad	isn't as... as...
la verdad es que	most of all
lo cierto es que	only
lo cual	other than that
más que nada	so that
no es tan... como...	the truth is that
para que	what is certain is that
solamente	which

Multiple Choice

1. Which does Melanie **not** say?

   a. The Mexican government is corrupt.   c. Many people are killed in drug wars.
   b. School violence is increasing.   d. The Mexican economy depends on
                                               tourism.

2. Melanie says the government ___ news about drug-trafficking related violence in order to ___.

   a. exaggerates   c. justify its tough policies on criminals
   b. downplays   d. protect Mexico's image

3. Whenever a cartel leader is killed or imprisoned, ___.

   a. drug prices increase in the U.S.   c. there is a sharp increase in violence
   b. the government runs a publicity   d. there is a noticeable decrease in violence
      campaign of its success on the war
      against the cartels

Text

La violencia y crimen en México es un tema muy controversial,	1	Violence and crime in Mexico is a very controversial issue,
ya que la economía del país depende del turismo,	2	because the economy of the country depends on tourism,
y muchos reportajes se han hecho en diferentes países sobre la violencia en México.	3	and many reports have been done in different countries about violence in Mexico.
La verdad es que el gobierno es muy corrupto y ha controlado los medios de comunicación,	4	The truth is that the government is very corrupt and has controlled the media,
para que no se exageren las noticias y no dar un mal aspecto o un mal concepto de México en el mundo.	5	so that they do not exaggerate the news or give a bad impression or a bad idea about Mexico to the world.
La verdad es que no sabemos exactamente qué es lo que pasa.	6	The truth is that we don't really know exactly what's going on.
lo cierto es que la violencia ha aumentado.	7	What is certain is that violence in Mexico has increased.
En realidad el crimen organizado, el narcotráfico y los esfuerzos por enfrentarlo, es lo que ha incrementado la violencia en México.	8	In reality, organized crime, drug trafficking and the efforts to tackle it, is what has increased violence in Mexico.
Más que nada cuando algún líder de algún cartel muere o es encerrado,	9	Most of all when any leader from any cartel dies or is imprisoned,
se dispara una guerra entre narcotraficantes de diferentes carteles,	10	it triggers a war between drug traffickers from different cartels,
y sí dejan diferent...- muchos muertos por la ciudad o en varias ciudades lo cual afecta el... el aspecto del país.	11	and they leave different... several dead in the city or in many cities, which affects... the look of the country.
Lo cierto es que solamente, esa... no solamente pero si la mayor parte del crimen en México, tiene que ver con el narcotráfico.	12	The truth is that only, that... not only but most of the crime in Mexico, is related to drug trafficking,.
De ahí en fuera es como en cualquier otro país.	13	Other than that it is just like in any other country.
La violencia en México eh... no es tan grave como aparenta ser.	14	Violence in Mexico uh... is not as serious as it appears to be.
De hecho eh... escuchado de casos más... de cosas más locas de otros países que no pasan en México.	15	Actually, uh... I've heard of cases... of crazier things in other countries that do not happen in Mexico.
En México en las escuelas no se ven pleitos, golpes, personas que meten armas a la escuela, o trabajos... o pleitos en el trabajo.	16	In Mexican schools you don't see fights, hitting, people bringing guns into school, or work... or fights at work.
Esas cosas no se ven en México. Ese tipo de violencia no es tanto en... en México.	17	You don't see those things in Mexico. That kind of violence isn't [found] that much in... in Mexico.
En las calles, en los carros, eso no pasa.	18	In the streets, in cars, that doesn't happen.
Simplemente las personas que tienen que ver con el narcotráfico o con algún tipo de crimen	19	Just people involved in drug trafficking or with any kind of organized crime are the ones involved in violence and crime.

organizado son las personas que están envueltas en la violencia y crimen.		
Lo que sí he notado en los últimos años es una gran mejoría por parte de... el gobierno y de los medios,	20	What I *have* noticed, in recent years, is a great improvement from the government and the media,
que se brinda más ayuda cuando hay casos de secuestros o violencia,	21	that offer more help in cases such as kidnapping or violence,
o por ejemplo el bullying por Internet o en las escuelas o de mujeres maltratadas.	22	for example, online bullying, or at school, or for abused women.
Ya ahorita hay mucha ayuda para las personas que sufren de esos tipos de violencia, y ya no se ven tantos casos.	23	Right now there's a lot of help for people who suffer that kind of violence, and we don't see that many cases anymore.
En ese aspecto sí ha mejorado mucho México en cuanto a la violencia y crimen.	24	In that respect, Mexico has greatly improved in terms of violence and crime.

Vocabulary

1. report[3] _____
2. the media[4] _____
3. to give a bad impression of[5] _____
4. to increase[7] _____
5. drug trafficking[8] _____
6. to address, tackle[8] _____
7. to imprison, lock up[9] _____
8. to have to do with[12] _____
9. serious[14] _____
10. argument, fight[16] _____
11. hit, blow, punch[16] _____
12. to offer, give[21] _____
13. kidnapping[21] _____
14. abused[22] _____

Translate

1. La economía depende *en el / del* turismo.
2. La verdad es que *es / sea* imposible resolver todos los problemas de la sociedad.
3. Su secuestro no tenía que *hacer / ver* nada con el narcotráfico.
4. Tales cosas simplemente no se *ve / ven* en el campo.
5. He notado una gran mejoría en los *últimos / recientes* meses.
6. Hay mucha ayuda *para / por* las mujeres maltratadas.

True or False: 1. T[7] 2. F[12] 3. F[16] 4. T[18-19] 5. T[20-23] **Expressions:** de ahí en fuera - other than that / de hecho - actually / en cuanto a - in terms of / en ese aspecto - in that respect / en los últimos años - in recent years / en realidad - in reality / la verdad es que - the truth is that / lo cierto es que - what is certain is that / lo cual - which / más que nada - most of all / no es tan... como... - isn't as... as... / para que - so that / solamente - only **Multiple Choice:** 1. b[2, 4, 11] 2. b, d[5] 3. c[9-10] **Vocabulary:** 1. reportaje 2. los medios (de comunicación) 3. dar un mal aspecto de 4. aumentar 5. narcotráfico 6. enfrentar 7. encerrar 8. tener que ver con 9. grave 10. pleito 11. golpe 12. brindarse 13. secuestro 14. maltratado **Translate:** 1. del[2] The economy depends on tourism. 2. es[4] The truth is that it's impossible to solve all of society's problems. 3. ver[12] His/Her kidnapping had nothing to do with drug trafficking. 4. ven[17] You just don't see such things in the countryside. 5. últimos[20] I've noticed a big improvement in recent months. 6. para[23] There's a lot of help for abused women.

notes

¿Español o Europeo?

Chelo (Spain)
267 words (137 wpm)   ⊙27

True or False

1. Most young Spaniards now agree that they feel more European than Spanish.   T ☐ F ☐
2. National sports teams are in part to thank for maintaining a Spanish identity.   T ☐ F ☐
3. The Erasmus program is designed to promote Spanish culture and identity.   T ☐ F ☐
4. Many young Spaniards go abroad to study or work.   T ☐ F ☐
5. Chelo says that she personally feels she is first Spanish, then European.   T ☐ F ☐

Expressions

a decir verdad	abroad
actualmente	although
aunque	and also
diría que	and so
el hecho de	be it; whether
en el extranjero	currently
en mi opinión	especially
incluso	even
muchas veces	for that reason
por lo que	I have to say; it's true that
por otra parte	I would say that
sí que es verdad que	in my opinion
sobre todo	often
y además	on the other hand
y así	the fact that
ya sea	to be honest

Multiple Choice

1. Chelo thinks young people in Spain today feel more ___, but ___.

   a. Spanish   c. do not realize it
   b. European   d. do not want to admit it

2. Chelo does **not** say that ___.

   a. many young people enjoy cultural   c. Spain wouldn't be the same without
       exchanges   Europe
   b. the European economy is bad   d. hosting the Olympics may bolster
       nowadays   national pride and identity

3. Chelo concludes that most young Spaniards feel ___.

   a. both Spanish and European   c. European more than Spanish
   b. Spanish more than European   d. like citizens of the world

Text

Preguntar a los jóvenes si se sienten europeos o españoles es una pregunta muy peliaguda,	1	Asking young people if they feel [more] European or Spanish is a tricky question,
sobre todo porque no se puede generalizar una respuesta	2	especially since you can not generalize an answer,
y cada persona piensa una cosa distinta, a decir verdad.	3	and everyone thinks something different, to be honest.
En mi opinión... en mi opinión, diría que... que creo que los jóvenes actuales españoles se sienten españoles,	4	In my opinion... in my opinion, I would say that... that I think young people in Spain these days feel Spanish,
aunque ellos muchas veces no se den cuenta.	5	even if they often don't realize it.
Yo creo que también ha favorecido mucho el hecho de tener una selección de fútbol española,	6	I also think that having a national soccer team contributes to this,
o una selección en cualquier deporte, ya sea olímpico, de competición...	7	or a team in any sport, be it Olympic, a competition...
Creo que el deporte en este caso ha ayudado mucho a identificarse como España.	8	I think that, here, sports have helped a lot in maintaining a Spanish identity.
Por otra parte, creo que los jóvenes españoles también se sienten europeos.	9	On the other hand, I think that young Spaniards also feel European.
Yo creo que España no sería nada sin Europa.	10	I don't think that Spain would be the same without Europe.
Por ejemplo, muchos de los jóvenes actualmente están disfrutando de programas europeos,	11	For example, many young Europeans are now enjoying programs,
como el programa Erasmus u otras becas que ofrece la Unión Europea para jóvenes.	12	such as the Erasmus program or other scholarships that the European Union offers to young people.
Y así tienen la posibilidad de estudiar en el extranjero, aprender idiomas, estar en contacto con otra cultura.	13	And so, they have the opportunity to study abroad, learn languages, experience another culture.
Creo que es una cosa muy positiva y que los jóvenes españoles están aprovechando muchísimo.	14	I think it's a very positive thing and that young Spaniards are taking advantage of these a lot.
Incluso muchas veces, creo que también se plantean trabajar o ir a estudiar toda la carrera, no solamente con este programa, fuera de España.	15	Often, even, I think that they consider working or going to do all their university studies, not just with this program, outside of Spain.
Sí que es verdad que la situación económica en Europa ahora no es la más propicia.	16	I have to say that the economic situation in Europe is not very favorable right now.
Pero por otra parte, creo que el intercambio cultural está favoreciendo muchísimo a que los jóvenes se sientan de verdad europeos,	17	But, on the other hand, I think that cultural exchanges are contributing to young people feeling truly European,
y yo creo que es un factor muy importante todo esto;	18	and I think that all this is an important factor.
por lo que diría que los jóvenes españoles se sienten españoles y, además, europeos.	19	For that reason, I would say that young Spaniards feel Spanish as well as European.

Vocabulary

1. youth, young people[1] _____
2. to feel[1] _____
3. tricky[1] _____
4. to realize[5] _____
5. to contribute to[6] _____
6. team[7] _____
7. scholarship[12] _____
8. to be in contact with[13] _____
9. to take advantage of[14] _____
10. to consider[15] _____
11. studies[15] _____
12. favorable[16] _____
13. exchange[17] _____

Translate

1. Me siento *como / -* ciudadano del mundo.
2. Cada *gente / persona* cree algo distinto.
3. Creo que también *ha / haya* favorecido mucho el hecho de ser parte de la Unión Europea.
4. Quiero aprovechar *de / -* esta oportunidad.
5. Me *planeo / planteo* estudiar en Nueva York el próximo año.
6. Muchos *españoles jóvenes / jóvenes españoles* trabajan fuera de España hoy en día.

---

notes

True or False: 1. F[3] 2. T[6-8] 3. F[13] 4. T[15] 5. F **Expressions:** a decir verdad - to be honest / actualmente - currently / aunque - although / diría que - I would say that / el hecho de - the fact that / en el extranjero - abroad / en mi opinión - in my opinion / incluso - even / muchas veces - often / por lo que - for that reason / por otra parte - on the other hand / sí que es verdad que - I have to say; it's true that / sobre todo - especially / y además - and also / y así - and so / ya sea - be it; whether **Multiple Choice:** 1. a[4], c[5] 2. d[10-12, 16] 3. a[19] **Vocabulary:** 1. jóvenes 2. sentirse 3. peliagudo 4. darse cuenta 5. favorecer 6. selección 7. beca 8. estar en contacto con 9. aprovechar 10. plantearse 11. carrera 12. propicio 13. intercambio **Translate:** 1. -[1] I feel like a citizen of the world. 2. -[3] Everyone thinks something different. 3. ha[6] I think that being a part of the European Union has contributed a lot to this, as well. 4. -[14] I want to take advantage of this opportunity. 5. planteo[15] I'm thinking about studying in New York next year. 6. jóvenes españoles9 A lot of young Spaniards (*or* young Spanish people, Spanish youth) work outside of Spain these days.

El Proceso de Paz

Felipe (Colombia)
353 words (142 wpm)   28

True or False

1. The Colombian government refuses to negotiate with FARC.   T ☐ F ☐
2. FARC has (or had) socialist and communist ideologies.   T ☐ F ☐
3. A peace treaty is currently being negotiated in Norway.   T ☐ F ☐
4. The peace process is controversial among Colombians.   T ☐ F ☐
5. Felipe is personally against the signing of the peace treaty.   T ☐ F ☐

Expressions

a pesar de que	after
a raíz de esto	along with
actualmente	also known as
al pasar de los años	as a result (of this)
bueno	at present
digamos que	despite that fact that
hace algunos años	finally
hoy en día	first of all
junto con	I personally believe that
lo dice todo	let's say that
luego de	more or less
más o menos	nowadays
por fin	over the years
primero que todo	says it all
también conocido como	some years ago
yo personalmente opino que	well

Multiple Choice

1. Felipe says that FARC ___.

   a. used to be known as the ELN   c. has been around for about 50 years
   b. is the key to peace in Colombia   d. is a communist party backed by Cuba

2. Which of the following is **not** true?

   a. FARC is a guerilla group.   c. The "Era of Violence" is in the past.
   b. The ELN is a guerilla group.   d. FARC continues to seek a communist
                                            revolution.

3. Felipe is against punishing FARC because ___.

   a. he agrees with their ideologies   c. they have changed their ideologies
   b. peace is more important   d. *none of the above*

Text

Bueno, un tema super importante en Colombia hoy en día es el proceso de paz.	1	Well, a super important issue in Colombia today is the peace process.
Eh… Se trata de las negociaciones que están haciendo el gobierno de Colombia con la guerrilla de las fuerzas armadas revolucionarias de Colombia, también conocidas como FARC.	2*	Uh… These are negotiations that are happening between the government of Colombia and the guerrillas of the Revolutionary Armed Forces of Colombia, also known as FARC.
Bueno, eh… primero que todo, esta guerrilla y junto con otra guerrilla que se llama el ELN existen más o menos hace cincuenta años.	3	Well, uh… first of all, this guerrilla group along with another guerrilla group called the ELN have been around more or less for 50 years.
Se formaron luego de la época de la violencia,	4	They were formed after "the era of violence",
que fue una época en la que los del Partido Liberal y los del Partido Conservador estaban en guerra.	5	which was a time when the Liberal Party and the Conservative Party were at war.
Y bueno, fue una época horrible,	6	And, well, it was a horrible time.
¿Por algo se llama la época de la violencia?	7	[I mean] Why is it called the era of violence?
El nombre lo dice todo.	8	The name says it all.
A raíz de esto, se formaron estas guerrillas	9	As a result of this, each of these guerrilla groups was formed
como una forma de oposición al sistema con ideologías comunistas y socialistas, cada una de ellas.	10	as a form of opposition to the system with socialist and communist ideologies, both of them.
Y, bueno, al pasar de los años—ya estamos hablando que han pasado cincuenta años desde su creación—	11	And, well, over the years—we're talking 50 years having passed since its inception—
digamos que los motivos de estas guerrillas ha cambiado	12	let's say that the motives of these guerrilla groups has changed
y ha dejado de ser como una revolución por buscar una Colombia mejor,	13	and no longer exist as a revolution for seeking a better Colombia;
y se ha convertido en un negocio.	14	[instead] having become a business.
Hace algunos años Noruega y Cuba em… sentaron las bases de lo que es hoy el proceso de paz,	15	Some years ago, Norway and Cuba um… laid the foundations of what is today the peace process,
y actualmente se están reuniendo en La Habana los líderes de la guerrilla, de la FARC específicamente,	16	and at present they are meeting in Havana with the guerrilla leaders, of the FARC specifically.
Se están reuniendo y están dialogando y están concretando eh… los pasos para por fin tener la paz en Colombia.	17	They are meeting and talking and laying out uh… the steps to finally have peace in Colombia.
Esto genera muchas reacciones en las personas de este país.	18	This generates many reactions among the people of this country.
Algunas personas no están de acuerdo con que se firme una paz,	19	Some people do not agree with the signing of a peace [treaty],
y se le permita a la guerrilla participar en política, por ejemplo.	20	and allowing the guerrilla group to participate in politics, for example.

Ellos lo que realmente quieren es que haya escarmiento o que haya castigo.	21	What they really want is that there be some discipline or punishment.
Y yo personalmente opino que es más importante la paz que la venganza,	22	Me, personally, I believe that peace is more important than revenge,
aunque... a pesar de que haya habido muchísimo dolor, muchísimo sufrimiento en este país a raíz de esta guerra.	23	even though... in spite of there having been so much pain, so much suffering in this country because of the war.
Creo que es más importante evitar más guerra.	24	I think it's more important to avoid more war.
Y creo que la gente debería tener eso más en cuenta,	25	And I think more people should take that into account more,
y pensar que es mucho más positivo y benéfico la paz ahora que la venganza.	26	and think that is much more positive and beneficial [to have] peace now than revenge.

*2 Whereas in English 'guerilla' is one person, in Spanish *guerilla* is a group of guerilla rebels, hence the use of the singular here.

Vocabulary

1. issue[1] _____
2. to be about[2] _____
3. guerrillas[2] _____
4. to be at war[5] _____
5. step[17] _____
6. to agree with[19] _____
7. lesson, warning[21] _____
8. punishment[21] _____
9. revenge[22] _____
10. to take into account[25] _____
11. beneficial[26] _____

Translate

1. La FARC *se / -* formó hace cincuenta años.
2. *A / De* raíz de esto, están en guerra.
3. Javier nunca ha dejado *a / de* compararse con su vecino.
4. Algunas personas no están *acuerdas / de acuerdo* con lo que pasó.
5. Yo personalmente opino que *es / sea* bastante importante.
6. Tuvimos en *cuenta / cuento* todos los hechos.

True or False: 1. F[2] 2. T[9-10] 3. F[16] 4. T[18] 5. F[22, 26] **Expressions:** a pesar de que - despite that fact that / a raíz de esto - as a result (of this) / actualmente - at present / al pasar de los años - over the years / bueno - well / digamos que - let's say that / hace algunos años - some years ago / hoy en día - nowadays / junto con - along with / lo dice todo - says it all / luego de - after / más o menos - more or less / por fin - finally / primero que todo - first of all / también conocido como - also known as / yo personalmente opino que - I personally believe that **Multiple Choice:** 1. c[3] 2. d[12-13] 3. b[22] **Vocabulary:** 1. tema 2. tratarse de 3. guerrilla 4. estar en guerra 5. paso 6. estar de acuerdo con 7. escarmiento 8. castigo 9. venganza 10. tener en cuenta 11. benéfico **Translate:** 1. se[4] FARC was formed fifty years ago. 2. a[9] As a result of this, they are at war. 3. de[13] Javier has never stopped comparing himself to his neighbor. 4. de acuerdo[19] Some people do not agree with what happened. 5. es[22] I personally think it's quite important. 6. cuenta[25] We took all the facts into account.

notes

La Realidad de Venezuela

True or False

1. Gisela is happy with Venezuela's progress in recent years.   T ☐ F ☐
2. The minimum wage is just enough to live on these days.   T ☐ F ☐
3. Many young people are now emigrating out of Venezuela.   T ☐ F ☐
4. Gisela quotes a saying that implies that all situations are temporary.   T ☐ F ☐
5. Gisela is optimistic about Venezuela's future.   T ☐ F ☐

Expressions

ahora bien	as a matter of fact
al pasar del tiempo	as time went by
así que	currently
cada vez	due to (the fact that)
de hecho	even
de repente	for whatever reason
debido a que	however
en estos momentos	irrespective of whether
hay que	more and more
hoy día	nowadays
inclusive	of course
independientemente de que	so; well
o sea que	so; therefore
por cualquier razón	suddenly
por supuesto	well anyway
pues	which means that
sin el temor de que	without fear of
y bueno	(you) have to

Multiple Choice

1. The basic family basket (*canasta básica familiar*) is the minimum monthly amount needed to provide for a family. According to Gisela, the basic family basket ___.

   a. doubled in the space of one year
   b. is nearly ten times the minimum wage
   c. has doubled since 1998
   d. is over 40,000 bolivars per month

2. What is **not** true about Venezuela's currency, the bolivar?

   a. It used to be the strongest currency in Latin America.
   b. Currency exchange is strongly controlled in Venezuela.
   c. It is pegged to the dollar.
   d. It is generally not accepted outside Venezuela.

3. Since the totalitarian regime took control of Venezuela's government, ___ increased.

   a. employment has
   b. crime rates have
   c. the value of the currency (*bolívar*) has
   d. *none of the above*

Text

Como tema social, eh... te quiero hablar un poquito de lo que está pasando en Venezuela en estos momentos.	1	For the social issue, uh... I want to tell you a bit about what is currently going on in Venezuela.
Desde el año mil novecientos noventa y ocho la situación política y social del país comenzó a cambiar,	2	In 1998 the political and social situation of the country started to change,
eh... debido a que tomó posesión un gobierno totalitario y con intenciones comunistas.	3	uh... due to a totalitarian regime taking control of the country and with communist intentions.
Este... muchos han estado de acuerdo con este régimen; otros no.	4	Uh... a lot of people were in favor of this regime; others weren't.
Muchos estuvieron de acuerdo en el momento de la votación,	5	Many supported [them] at the time of the elections,
pero al pasar del tiempo cuando se dieron cuenta que el gobierno era realmente un gobierno totalitario y comunista.	6	but as time went by, they became aware that the government was really a totalitarian communist regime.
Pues, no quisieron seguir apoyándolo.	7	So, they didn't want to support it any longer.
Eh... ahora bien, independientemente de que muchos estén de acuerdo con ese régimen y otros no,	8	Uh... now, irrespective of whether many may support this regimen and others not,
la realidad hoy día en Venezuela es que diecisiete años después que este régimen toma posesión del gobierno,	9	the truth today in Venezuela is that seventeen years after this regime took control of the government,
los niveles de la delincuencia cada vez son mayores;	10	the crime levels are higher and higher;
las estadísticas, inclusive el año pasado en el año dos mil catorce, arrojaron que hubo más de veintitrés mil muertos sólo por violencia.	11	the statistics, even last year in 2014, showed that there had been over 23,000 deaths just by violence,
O sea que la inseguridad en el país es altísima.	12	which means that the lack of safety in the country is very high.
Uno no puede salir a la calle libremente sin el temor de que de repente al cruzar la esquina de puedan matar.	13	One cannot freely go out on the streets without the fear of being killed as one turns the corner.
Es sumamente inseguro.	14	It's extremely unsafe.
El índice laboral, por supuesto, ha ido cada vez empeorando más y más.	15	The employment index of course has been getting worse and worse.
La inflación ha ido cada vez aumentando más y más.	16	Inflation has been steadily increasing.
De hecho, actualmente el sueldo mínimo en Venezuela es aproximadamente cinco mil seiscientos bolívares.	17*	As a matter of fact, currently the [monthly] minimum wage is 5,600 bolívares.
Y el costo de la "cesta básica", que es lo que llaman normalmente ca-... "la canasta básica familiar", tiene un costo de casi veinte mil bolívares,	18	And the cost of the ba-... "basic basket", or what is usually called "the basic family basket", has a cost of 20,000 bolívares,

que subió de hecho... del año dos mil catorce al año dos mil quince subió en más de un cien por ciento.	19	which is increased as a matter of fact... from 2014 to 2015 it increased in more than 100%.
Así que te podrás imaginar, pues, como está la situación financiera y social para la gente en Venezuela.	20	So you can imagine uh... how the financial and social situation for people in Venezuela must be.
Eh... esa es la realidad de Venezuela.	21	Uh... that's Venezuela's reality.
La realidad de Venezuela es que hace poco menos de veinte años era el país número uno de América Latina con su moneda, que es el bolívar, muy fuerte, bastante fuerte.	22	The reality of Venezuela is that less than 20 years ago it was the #1 country in Latin America for its currency, the bolivar, [which was] very strong, quite strong.
Y ahora es el último país de América Latina con una moneda, un bolívar, que no vale absolutamente nada,	23	And now it is the last country in Latin America, with a currency, a bolivar, that doesn't have any value at all,
y que no es aceptado en ninguna parte del mundo.	24	and is not accepted in any part of the world.
Eh... en Venezuela hay un fuerte control cambiario y... y bueno.	25	Uh... in Venezuela there is a strong currency exchange control and... well anyway.
Toda esta situación eh... ha incrementado significativamente los índices de migración de las familias...	26	This whole situation uh... has significantly increased the migration of families...
de familias enteras, este... especialmente de nuestros jóvenes.	27	of entire families, uh... and especially of our youngsters.
Los jóvenes siempre se consideran la sangre de un país, el futuro de un país,	28	Young people are always considered the blood of a country, the future of a country,
y muy tristemente nuestros jóvenes profesionales este... se han ido; se han estado yendo del país.	29	and very sadly our young professionals uh... have left; they've been getting out of the country.
Y bueno... hoy día están regados por todo el mundo,	30	And today they are scattered all over the world,
em... Estados Unidos, Europa, Australia y otros países de Latinoamérica.	31	um... the US, Europe, Australia and other Latin American countries.
Eh... realmente es una situación muy triste, eh... pero es nuestra realidad actual y... hay que aceptarla.	32	Uh... it's really a very sad situation, uh... but this is our current reality, and... we must accept it.
Hay un dicho muy criollo que dice:	33	There is a local saying that goes:
"No hay mal que dure cien años, ni cuerpo que lo resista".	34	"There is no evil that lasts a hundred years, nor body that can withstand it."
Eso es un dicho muy criollo en Venezuela.	35	This is a very local saying in Venezuela.
Y todos los venezolanos que estamos fuera del país,	36	And all Venezuelans that are out of the country,
y los que eligieron quedarse por cualquier razón,	37	and those that have chosen to stay for whatever reason,
conservamos la esperanza de que Venezuela pueda recuperarse algún día.	38	we [all] maintain the hope that Venezuela will be able to recover some day.
No sabemos cuánto tiempo va a tomar,	39	We don't know how long it will take,
pero no perdemos la esperanza de que eso suceda.	40	but we don't lose hope that this will happen.

Vocabulary

1. to go along with[4] _____
2. elections[5] _____
3. crime[10] _____
4. to show that[11] _____
5. to go outside[13] _____
6. extremely[14] _____
7. employment index[15] _____
8. minimum wage[17] _____
9. currency[22] _____
10. to be scattered[30] _____
11. saying[33] _____
12. native, local[33] _____
13. to recover, get better[38] _____

Translate

1. Comencé *aprendiendo / a aprender* alemán hace seis meses.
2. Es sumamente inseguro *a / -* salir a la calle hoy en día.
3. Cuesta cuatro *mil / miles* cincocientos bolívares.
4. Gisela dice que el bolívar *no / -* vale absolutamente nada.
5. Hoy día muchos jóvenes venezolanos están *regados / regando* por todo el mundo.
6. Ha logrado lo que nadie imaginó, debido a que *tuvo / tuviera* mucha suerte.

notes

True or False: 1. F 2. F[17-18] 3. T[29] 4. T[33-34] 5. T[38-40] **Expressions:** ahora bien - however / al pasar del tiempo - as time went by / así que - so / cada vez - more and more / de hecho - as a matter of fact / de repente - suddenly / debido a que - due to (the fact that) / en estos momentos - currently / hay que - (you) have to / hoy día - nowadays / inclusive - even / independientemente de que - irrespective of whether / o sea que - which means that / por cualquier razón - for whatever reason / por supuesto - of course / pues - so / sin el temor de que - without fear of / y bueno - well anyway **Multiple Choice:** 1. a[19] 2. c[22, 24-25] 3. b[9-10] **Vocabulary:** 1. estar de acuerdo con 2. votación 3. delincuencia 4. arrojar que 5. salir a la calle 6. sumamente 7. índice laboral 8. sueldo mínimo 9. moneda 10. estar regado 11. dicho 12. criollo 13. recuperarse **Translate:** 1. a aprender[2] I started learning German six months ago. 2. - It isn't safe to leave the house these days. 3. mil[17] It costs 4,600 bolivars. 4. no[23] Gisela says that the bolivar isn't worth a thing. 5. regados[30] Nowadays, many young Venezuelans are scattered all over the world. 6. tuvo[3] He/She accomplished what nobody had imagined, due to the fact that he had a lot of luck.

La Educación en Chile

Jaime (Chile)
461 words (154 wpm)

⊘ 30

True or False

1. Jaime is proud of the education system in his country. T ☐ F ☐
2. He explains the correlation between income and the quality of education. T ☐ F ☐
3. P.S.U. is an ivy league college in Chile. T ☐ F ☐
4. In Chile, studying education is as prestigiou as studying medicine or law. T ☐ F ☐
5. Jaime talks about his personal experience with getting into college and choosing a major. T ☐ F ☐

Expressions

a veces	depending on
además	for the most part
así que	for up to two years
de acuerdo a	in many cases
durante hasta dos años	moreover
en cuanto a	on the other hand
en muchos casos	since; because
entre más... mejor...	so; therefore
entre menos... peor...	sometimes
es decir	that is to say
la mayoría de los casos	the less... the worse...
lo que se traduce que	the more... the better...
por lo tanto	therefore
por otra parte	when it comes to
ya que	which means that

Multiple Choice

1. The minimum wage in Chile is ___.

   a. around 200,000 pesos
   b. over 500,000 pesos
   c. between 200,000 and 500,000 pesos
   d. *He doesn't say.*

2. Jaime argues that the quality of education in public schools is low because ___.

   a. classes are sometimes canceled
   b. the teachers are not very good
   c. the requirements are low
   d. *all of the above*

3. Jaime says that college loans from the government ___ and ___.

   a. are only available to families with strong credit histories
   b. can take up to 20 years to pay off
   c. would help correct the disadvantage those from lower income families face
   d. *none of the above*

Text

La educación en Chile diría yo que es uno de los temas más controversiales durante la última década.	1	Education in Chile, I would say, has been one of the most controversial issues over the last decade.
Existe una diferencia demasiado marcada en cuanto a la calidad de educación que reciben las distintas clases sociales.	2	There is a very noticeable difference when it comes to education that the different social classes get.
Bueno, esto debe pasar en muchos países.	3	Well, this must happen in many countries.
Pero entre más ingresos tiene una familia, mejor es la educación que recibe,	4	But the higher the income a family has, the better the education they receive,
y entre menos ingresos tenga, peor es la educación que recibe.	5	and the lower the income they have, the worse the education they receive.
Esto ha provocado que cada año salgan los estudiantes a manifestarse en las calles,	6	This has resulted in students going out to demonstrate in the streets every year,
para exigir mejoras en la educación, mayor calidad, oportunidades iguales para todos.	7	to demand improvements in education, better quality, equal opportunities for all.
Por ejemplo, la educación en Chile es muy muy cara.	8	For instance, education in Chile is very, very expensive.
El sueldo mínimo en Chile es aproximadamente 200.000 pesos.	9	The minimum wage in Chile is around 200,000 pesos.
Y un programa de educación superior vale sobre 200.000 pesos;	10	and a higher education program can cost over 200,000 pesos;
puede valer 200.000, 300.000, 400.000, hasta 500.000.	11	it can cost 200,000, 300,000, 400,000, even 500,000.
Y eso es lo que reclaman los estudiantes en Chile,	12	And that's what students are demanding in Chile,
que la educación es un lucro y no un derecho como debiera ser.	13	that education now is profit and not a right as it should be.
Por otra parte, para ingresar a la universidad, hay una prueba llamada P.S.U.	14	On the other hand, to get into college, there is an exam called P.S.U.
Y puedes optar a distintas carreras de acuerdo al puntaje que obtuviste.	15	And you can choose different majors depending on the score you got.
Y cada año se repite la misma historia:	16	And every year the same story is repeated:
los que tienen menores puntajes corresponden a aquellos que estudiaron en colegios estatales,	17	those with lower scores correspond to those who studied in state schools,
es decir, de familias que tienen menores ingresos.	18	that is to say, from families with lower incomes.
Y los que tienen mayores puntajes son aquellos que estudiaron en colegios particulares que son los más caros.	19	And those with the highest scores are those who studied in private schools that are the most expensive.
La calidad de la educación en colegios estatales es bastante menor.	20	The quality of education in public schools is much lower.
A veces las clases no se hacen,	21	Sometimes students don't have their lessons,
hay horas perdidas, los niveles de exigencia son menores,	22	there are missing hours, the requirements are lower,

lo que se traduce que finalmente aquellos estudiantes que estudiaron en esos colegios tendrán menores puntajes en la prueba P.S.U.	23	which means that eventually those students who studied in these schools have lower test scores in the P.S.U.
Por lo tanto, en la mayoría de los casos, no les alcanza el puntaje para estudiar lo que ellos quieren.	24	Therefore, for the most part, they will not obtain the score they need to study what they want.
Otro problema es la poca valoración que se tiene de la carrera pedagogía,	25	Another problem is the low value that a an education major gets,
así que los estudiantes que tienen buenos niveles de educación, no optan por esta carrera,	26	so students with high level of education don't choose this major,
ya que no está muy bien vista en nuestra sociedad.	27	since our society doesn't view it very favorably.
Siempre prefieren medicina, odontología, derecho, las carreras típicas que están bien vistas.	28	They always prefer medicine, dentistry, law, typical majors that are viewed favorably.
Además, hay muchas universidades que imparten la carrera de pedagogía,	29	Moreover, there are many universities where you can get a degree in education,
y con niveles que no son los adecuados.	30	but with levels that aren't adequate,
Por lo tanto, los profesores que egresan de esas universidades, en muchos casos, no tienen las competencias necesarias para realizar clases a estudiantes de educación básica y media.	31	Therefore, teachers who graduate from those universities, in many cases, do not have the necessary skills to teach students in primary and secondary school.
Además, hay un crédito universitario que otorga el estado.	32	Additionally, there's a college loan that the government grants to students,
y es para quienes no pueden pagar completamente su carrera.	33	and it is for those who cannot fully pay for their studies.
Y una vez que dejas de estudiar y comienzas a trabajar, debes empezar a pagar este crédito durante hasta veinte años de tu vida,	34	And once you stop studying and start working, you must start paying the loan for up to twenty years of your life,
y pagando incluso el doble o triple del dinero prestado inicialmente.	35	and even pay two or three times the original loan.
Y esto hace pensar a los estudiantes que el estado ve la educación como un negocio y no un derecho.	36	And this suggests to students that the state sees education as a business and not a right.

Vocabulary

1. noticeable[2] _____
2. income[4] _____
3. to result in[6] _____
4. to demonstrate, protest[6] _____
5. to demand[7] _____
6. improvement[7] _____
7. wage[9] _____
8. profit[13] _____
9. exam[14] _____
10. to choose, select[15] _____
11. score[17] _____
12. private school[19] _____
13. public school[20] _____
14. to reach, obtain[24] _____
15. valuation, esteem[25] _____
16. dentistry[28] _____
17. (study of) law[28] _____
18. to be viewed favorably[28] _____
19. to graduate from[31] _____
20. college loan[32] _____
21. to borrow[35] _____

Translate

1. Es *un / una* tema muy controversial.
2. Esto ha provocado que *es / sea* imposible alcanzar un acuerdo.
3. Eso se traduce que *van / vayan* a manifestarse para exigir mejoras en sus sueldos.
4. No hemos optado *por / -* hacer eso.
5. Este estudiante todavía no ha demostrado que tiene *la competencia necesaria / las competencias necesarias* para egresar de la universidad.
6. Una vez que *dejamos / dejemos* de exigir nuestros derechos, vamos a perder lo poco que tenemos ahora.

---

notes

True or False: 1. F 2. T[19-20, 24] 3. F[14] 4. F[25, 28] 5. F **Expressions:** a veces - sometimes / además - moreover / así que - so; therefore / de acuerdo a - depending on / durante hasta veinte años - for up to twenty years / en cuanto a - when it comes to / en muchos casos - in many cases / entre más... mejor... - the more... the better... / entre menos... peor... - the less... the worse... / es decir - that is to say / la mayoría de los casos - for the most part / lo que se traduce que - which means that / por lo tanto - therefore / por otra parte - on the other hand / ya que - since; because **Multiple Choice:** 1. a[9] 2. d[21-22, 31] 3. b[34] **Vocabulary:** 1. marcado 2. ingresos 3. provocar que 4. manifestarse 5. exigir 6. mejora 7. sueldo 8. lucro 9. prueba 10. optar a 11. puntaje 12. colegio particular 13. colegio estatal 14. alcanzar 15. valoración 16. odontología 17. derecho 18. estar bien visto 19. egresar de 20. crédito universitario 21. prestart **Translate:** 1. un[1] It's a very controversial topic. 2. sea[6] This has made it impossible to reach an agreement. 3. van[23] That means that they'll protest to demand improvements in their wages. 4. por[26] We haven't chosen to do that. 5. las competencias necesarias[31] This student has not yet demonstrated that he has the necessary skills to graduate from university. 6. dejamos[34] Once we stop demanding our rights, we'll lose what little we have now.

notes

Visit our website for information on current and upcoming titles,

free excerpts, and language learning resources.

www.lingualism.com